RASULULLAH

Selected Hadith from the Life of the Prophet Muhammad ﷺ (SAW)

▶ Commentaries
▶ Emphasis on Contemporary Topics
▶ Islam through the Teachings of Rasulullah ﷺ

Dr. Muhammad Yunus Kumek

Medina House ⁰
publishing

Cover Images: Courtesy of Masjid Nabawi, Medina (Al-Madinah).
Photo taken by Y. Kumek.
Interior Background: Green carpet design with the courtesy of
Masjid Nabawi, Medina (Al-Madinah). Photo taken by Y. Kumek.

Medina Houseᶜ
publishing

www.medinahouse.org
170 Manhattan Ave, Po. Box 63
Buffalo, New York, 14215
contact@medinahouse.org

Published in the United States of America.

CONTENTS

Selected Hadith with Commentaries

Allah ﷻ

> *Belief in Allah سبحانه وتعالى has more than 70 branches.*
> *The highest level as a sign of belief is accepting the*
> *statement that "there is no deity except only One God."*
> *The lowest sign of belief is to remove a harmful object*
> *from the road (5).*

1. Belief in Allah سبحانه وتعالى has more than 70 branches. The highest level as a sign of belief is accepting the statement that "there is no deity except Allah سبحانه وتعالى." The lowest sign of belief is to remove a harmful object from the road (5).

Commentary

A person who has a belief in Allah سبحانه وتعالى can have different signs of this belief. The highest sign of this belief is one's clear proclamation, saying, and accepting the statement that there is no deity or anything to worship, fear or attach except and only to and from One God. One of the lower signs of this belief can be doing something good and ethical for others. This person may or may not have an explicit belief in God but doing something good brings the person closer to Allah سبحانه وتعالى at a personal experience. Because all the sources of good and beneficial actions and deeds are from Allah سبحانه وتعالى. All the sources of evil and destruction are due to the person's evil self and Satan. The above is an example of a good action such as removing a harmful object or item on a road that could possibly harm others.

2. Evil and God: Rasulullah ﷺ practiced to read the prayer of tahiyyat in the last portion of each prayer. This prayer translates as "All the good, the pure, and the blessed is from Allah سبحانه وتعالى and in its essence belongs to Allah سبحانه وتعالى."

Commentary

It is important to know in Islamic theology that Allah سبحانه وتعالى is the source of all good. All the sources of evil are the person himself or herself. It can also be due to the evil caused by other humans or unseen beings such as Satan. Therefore, there is no blame to Allah سبحانه وتعالى in any occurrence of evil. Rasulullah ﷺ instructs to read this very important notion in each prayer to remove the bad and blame related imaginations about Allah سبحانه وتعالى in one's personal relationship with the Divine. Muslims are required to read the above statement at least once in each prayer of the five daily prayers. In Muslim practice, tahiyyat and salawat, sending blessings to Rasulullah ﷺ always bring peace, tranquility in this life and pleasure of Allah سبحانه وتعالى. Therefore, Muslims chant and read tahiyyat and salawat a lot every day, especially on Fridays.

---

3. Evil and God: Anas narrated that the Prophet Muhammad ﷺ's son Ibrahim was about to die. Rasulullah ﷺ embraced his son and said "this is the will of Allah سبحانه وتعالى." Anas said "the boy was taking his last few breaths in life while Rasulullah ﷺ was hugging him." Rasulullah ﷺ was crying and shed tears and said: "Oh Ibrahim, our eyes are filled with tears and our heart is filled with grief, but we do not say anything except Our Merciful Nourishing God is pleased. Indeed, oh Ibrahim! we are grieved over our loss. [2] (2315)."

Commentary

Above is a narration about the Prophet Muhammad ﷺ's loss of his son who was six to seven months old. This incident shows the human qualities of Rasulullah ﷺ. Rasulullah ﷺ was a human being. When there is a loss it is normal to grieve and be sad over the deceased. As a role model, Rasulullah ﷺ again sets the boundaries of humanness within the observance of respect to the Divine Will in the utmost evil-seeming difficult situations. Rasulullah ﷺ specifically mentions that he grieves but he does not complain. Rasulullah ﷺ is not in the mode of blame in the encounters of destiny designated by Allah سبحانه وتعالى. In another narration of the same incident, one person observing the

Prophet's crying over his son and was surprised and said "are you also crying?" The Prophet mentioned that he was a human being and it was normal to grieve within the limits of keeping respect to the Divine Will of Allah سبحانه وتعالى.

4. Allah سبحانه وتعالى is kind and loves kindness. Allah سبحانه وتعالى rewards kindness but not harshness. Allah سبحانه وتعالى does not accept and reward anything but kindness [2] (2593).

Commentary

Above testimony from Rasulullah ﷺ shows the notion of what is accepted and rewarded by Allah سبحانه وتعالى in our humanly defined "good, ethical and moral" actions. In this perspective, one can see that the internal disposition of a person with humbleness and kindness are some of the key traits of a person when engaging in different social discourses. To prove this point, one of the verses in the Quran [2:263] mentions this very clearly that if one is going to give charity in a harsh or arrogant attitude, it is better for this person not to give any monetary help to others but first to be nice, gentle and kind in verbal discourse. In other words, the best way is to give charity with a manner of humbleness and kindness. Allah سبحانه وتعالى appreciates the state of the heart and the attitude of caring and kindness towards others but not the outcomes usually applauded by humans.

5. There was a man walking on the road. Then, he found a harmful thing on the road that can potentially harm people. He then put this item on the side of the road so that it would not harm people. Allah سبحانه وتعالى accepted his sincere action and forgave his sins [2] (1914R1).

Commentary

One can see that there are different representations of the belief in Allah سبحانه وتعالى. A person who does service to benefit others can be granted forgiveness and pardon by Allah سبحانه وتعالى and enter Heaven after death. This good deed can be as small as removing a harmful object from the path of people as mentioned in the above testimony of Rasulullah ﷺ. One should construct the knowledge about Allah سبحانه وتعالى in Islam with the teachings of the Quran and through the testimonies of Rasulullah ﷺ. God or Allah in Arabic in Islam is loving, caring, appreciative, forgiving as well as just, active, watching, interfering, listening but acting with wisdom not with the immediate desires of humans. Allah سبحانه وتعالى as in the above case always presents numerous avenues for people to walk and get close to in the Divine relationship either through service, altruism, worship, good word, or a smile towards other fellows. All actions have value with an initial step that the person first recognizes and appreciates the One and only Creator.

6. Allah سبحانه وتعالى is kind and loves kindness. Allah سبحانه وتعالى showers blessings on kindness but not on harshness [1] (4807).

Commentary

In the above testimony of Rasulullah ﷺ, Allah سبحانه وتعالىis kind, caring, gentle and treats all the creation with kindness and gentleness. When a person has this quality, then Allah سبحانه وتعالى showers the blessings on his or her life with good achievements. One of the praiseworthy and well-known traits of the Prophet Muhammad ﷺ is being extremely gentle, kind and caring. The Quran mentions[1] that one of the reasons why billions of people have been following the teachings of Rasulullah ﷺ is due to his trait of kindness.

---

1. [3:159]

7. When Allah سبحانه وتعالى loves a person, Allah سبحانه وتعالى calls
    Gabriel and tells: I love this person. Love this person. Rasulullah
    ﷺ said: "Then, Gabriel loves this person." Then, Gabriel makes an
    announcement in the skies and says: "Allah سبحانه وتعالى loves this
    person, I love this person." Then, the inhabitants of the skies love
    this person. Then, this person is given acceptance and honor on
    the earth [2] (2637).

Commentary

Above is a narration that shows the gist of one's intention in all affairs of
life. If a person does everything to please Allah سبحانه وتعالى then there
is a love bestowed from Allah سبحانه وتعالى to this person. When Allah
سبحانه وتعالى loves and is pleased with a person then, the love of others
follows. In this regard, it is wrong and lowly to seek the love and pleasure
of others except Allah سبحانه وتعالى because all the creation is limited.
There are always disappointments when a person does something
to please someone. In the relationship with Allah سبحانه وتعالى, Allah
سبحانه وتعالى appreciates and recompenses a reward in the form of others
loving this person as well.

8. Rasulullah ﷺ narrated that Allah سبحانه وتعالى said "I am close to
    My servant's thoughts about what he or she thinks about Me [2]
    (2675)."

Commentary

Above is the announcement of Allah سبحانه وتعالى about the importance
of one's positive and good assumptions about Allah سبحانه وتعالى.
Especially, in the renderings of theodicy, if a person is always in a blame
mode to God for the encounters of evil, it cannot be a good assumption
but unfruitful disposition for the person. Therefore, a person in Islam is
always required to have a good opinion, assumption and expectation of

Allah سبحانه وتعالى in this world and afterlife. Then, Allah سبحانه وتعالى treats the person according to this person's good, positive, and constructive relationship, feelings and thoughts about Allah سبحانه وتعالى. However, if the person is always in blame mode and expects nothing after death, then the person can possibly end up in a situation according to how he or she portrays God in one's mind and heart.

9. Rasulullah ﷺ narrated that Allah سبحانه وتعالى said "I am close to My servant's thoughts about what he or she thinks about Me. I am with this person when he or she calls Me. If one calls Me in oneself, then I call him or her in Myself. If one glorifies Me in a gathering then, I honor this person in a much better gathering. If one comes close to Me a hand's distance, I come close this person an arm's distance. If one comes close to Me an arm's distance, I come close to this person a fathom's distance. If one comes close to Me walking, I come close to this person running [2] (2675)."

Commentary

Above is the continuation of the previous narration which has a clear metaphorical and figurative language. The essence of the above narration explains that when a person makes an effort of establishing relationship with Allah سبحانه وتعالى, then Allah سبحانه وتعالى appreciates that and makes it easy for this person. Allah سبحانه وتعالى is above and beyond from human renderings of distance, walking, or running. In the Quran and sayings of Rasulullah ﷺ, sometimes there is metaphorical language to make the people understand a message easy and personalize it in one's relationship with Allah سبحانه وتعالى. In the encounters of theodicy or evil, one can understand from above narration that Allah سبحانه وتعالى always appreciates and responds to human's genuine efforts to establish relationship with their Creator. Therefore, Allah سبحانه وتعالى is always Present, Alive, Active, Interfering and Forgiving.

10. Rasulullah ﷺ said: Allah ﷻ has 99 Names. Whoever memorizes and reads them enters Heaven. Allah ﷻ is Unique, One and Odd, not like humans. Therefore, Allah ﷻ likes odd numbers, [2] (2677) (2677R1).

Commentary

Above testimony of Rasulullah ﷺ is very critical in acquiring the true knowledge of Allah ﷻ. There are different Names and Attributes of Allah ﷻ. One can approximate one's correct understanding about God by studying these Divine Names. Therefore, there is an encouragement to memorize and to chant those names constantly in different encounters of life due to the above narration of Rasulullah ﷺ. In the other portion of the narration, there is an emphasis and reminder about the Uniqueness and Oneness of Allah ﷻ unlike humans with the wrong concepts of anthropomorphism. The notion of odd numbers signifies this critical fact in one's daily life. An even number can signify the human concepts of divisibility, spouse, partner, and equability. Due to this narration, it is a common practice among Muslims to memorize the Names of Allah ﷻ and chant them regularly.

11. None of you should pray to Allah ﷻ as: Oh Allah ﷻ! Forgive me if you want. Oh Allah ﷻ! Have mercy on me if you want." Rasulullah ﷺ continued: One should not be hesitant when one prays to Allah ﷻ but be insistent and persistent in prayers to Allah ﷻ. Indeed, Allah ﷻ is the Doer of everything. Allah ﷻ can do whatever Allah ﷻ wants and wills. There is no one to force Allah ﷻ [2] (2677R1).

Commentary

Above is an example of the misconstructions about the knowledge of Allah ﷻ. In the boundaries of humans and Allah ﷻ, one should understand that a person cannot humanize literally one's relationship with Allah ﷻ. As in the above example, when one asks something from another person there is always the possibility of the request not to be fulfilled due to limited abilities of a person or due unexpected changing circumstances. This is not valid for God. Allah 📿 is the All Powerful. In that sense, in Islam, it is very critical to have proper etiquette of relationship, adab, with Allah 📿. A person is expected to be humble, beg, be insistent and persistent in one's request from Allah 📿. Especially, in the dispositions of forgiveness and asking for mercy that is one of the essentials to have in one's relationship with Allah 📿.

12. Whoever loves and looks forward to meeting with Allah 📿, Allah 📿 loves to meet with this person. Whoever is not eager to meet with Allah 📿, Allah 📿 is not pleased to meet with this person [2] (2683).

Commentary

Above is the testimony of Rasulullah 📿 about the desired state of one's relationship with Allah 📿. Although one should desire to live a long life as mentioned in another narration of Rasulullah 📿 [2], one should always see death as a means of meeting with the Beloved, Allah 📿, Who the person is looking forward to meeting. One should see death as a means of meeting with a Friend who the person missed so much and looked forward to meeting. This is a goal in one's spiritual state and belief in Allah 📿 to achieve in one's life. Rasulullah 📿 teaches Muslims to ask for this state in their prayers as "Oh Allah 📿, please give me the spiritual state of heart and mind that I would like to meet with you [3]"

13. Aisha, the wife of Rasulullah 📿 said: "Whoever loves and looks forward to meeting with Allah 📿, Allah 📿 loves to meet with this person. Whoever is not eager to meet with Allah 📿, Allah 📿 is not pleased to meet with this person." Then, I said to Rasulullah 📿: "Oh Messenger of Allah 📿! if it is a dislike about death, we all have this feeling." Then, Rasulullah 📿 said: "it is not that, but when a person has a belief, appreciation, and gratitude for Allah 📿 in one's life, then glad tidings of the mercy, love and Heaven are given at the time of death to this person, and this person desires

to meet with Allah ﷻ. When a person who does not have belief, appreciation, and gratitude for Allah ﷻ then, this person is given the bad news of the accountability and displeasure of Allah ﷻ at the time of death, then this person is not eager to meet with Allah ﷻ [2] (2684).

Commentary

One can see from the above testimony of Rasulullah ﷺ that everyone is going to know their situation in afterlife immediately during and after death. At this time, depending on the type of the news that the person would receive, either the person would be eager to meet with Allah ﷻ or not. In addition, as one can understand that the life is a trial and test for a person in Islam. In this perspective, the person immediately receives the result of one's lifelong struggle at the verge of death immediately. Also, one can see the type of interaction of Rasulullah ﷺ with his wife and other Muslims. There is always the case of learning and teaching. Especially, in this case, the wife of Rasulullah ﷺ, Aisha, immediately asks if there is anything that is not clear without reservation. It is actually narrated the wife of Rasulullah ﷺ Aisha had a very strong and inspiring character in her interaction with Rasulullah ﷺ. She did not make any reservations if there were any issues to be raised. Yet, Rasulullah ﷺ always publicly and privately expressed his immense love towards Aisha. After the demise of Rasulullah ﷺ, as there were some disputes among the Muslims, Aisha had her own disposition and led an army herself as the commander in chief in order to defend her disposition.

14. One day, Rasulullah ﷺ visited a Muslim who became extremely sick, lost his power and became so thin. Rasulullah ﷺ said to him: "Did you supplicate to Allah ﷻ or asked or prayed for this sickness?". The sick man said: "Yes. I used to pray to Allah ﷻ as: Oh Allah ﷻ! If there is punishment waiting for me after I die, please give it to me and make it quick in this world." Rasulullah ﷺ said: "Glory be to Allah ﷻ! You cannot handle and bear it. Why don't you pray to Allah ﷻ as: Oh Allah ﷻ! Give me good, easiness and blessings in this world and in the afterlife, and protect me from

punishment!" The man said it and prayed to Allah ﷻ as Rasulullah ﷺ suggested, then the man restored his good health [2] (2687).

Commentary

In the above narration, Rasulullah ﷺ teaches Muslims the etiquettes of one's relation with Allah ﷻ and how to pray and ask for one's needs. As Rasulullah ﷺ is instructed by Allah ﷻ to always show the easy way for humans, Rasulullah ﷺ teaches how to always ask easiness and goodness from Allah ﷻ in this life and after death. In another perspective, one can see the power of prayer so that when a person calls Allah ﷻ sincerely, the person's prayer is immediately answered. On another note, one can see that the early Muslims as the early students of Islam were guided through Rasulullah ﷺ in their engagement with Allah ﷻ. Perhaps, in this case as similar to many other cases, the Prophet Muhammad ﷺ was informed about this man by Allah ﷻ and Rasulullah ﷺ visited this sick man. Then, this was a teaching opportunity for all Muslims at that time and for the generations to follow.

15. Allah ﷻ has mobile angels that only follow, attend, and are present in the circles and groups of worship, glorification and remembrance of Allah ﷻ. When they find such a group or circle, they sit with them. Then, they surround this group with their wings until the space is filled between them the sky and the earth. When the people leave, the angels ascend and take off to the sky. Then, Allah ﷻ, the Exalted and the Glorious, although Allah ﷻ knows where they were, asks them: "Where are you coming from?" The angels reply: "we are coming from Your creation on the earth. They were praying, worshipping, and chanting to You with the phrases of perfection of Your Glory and removing all the wrong thoughts and feelings in their relationship with You[2], with a phrase of exalting Your Name[3], with a phrase of proclaiming Your Oneness, Uniqueness and Distinctiveness as the Creator[4], with an expression of gratitude and appreciation of all Your bounties[5], [2] (2689).

2. SubhanAllah
3. Allahuakbar
4. La ilaha illa Allah
5. Alhamdulillah

Commentary

Allah ﷻ knows everything. Allah ﷻ makes angels witness everything such as humans' actions so that when people face Allah ﷻ in afterlife at the time of accountability, the person has a fair judgment with witnesses. In addition, as a teaching method for both humans and angels, in the above narration, there is the dialogue between angels and Allah ﷻ about a group of people who are sincerely worshipping Allah ﷻ with their chants, glorifications and gratitude. This testimony also can allude to the fact that there are the authentic phrases of chants and meditation that are approved and revealed by Allah ﷻ. In the engagements with different religions, the question of authenticity is always there. In this case, the specific phrases that are derived from this narration are "SubhanAllah, Allahuakbar, La ilaha illa Allah, Alhamdulillah, and Astagfirullah." Therefore, it is important to engage oneself with the original phrases which are authenticated by Allah ﷻ in Islam. Although there is always the real state of the heart while one is chanting these phrases, the sincere stance of the heart with external correct expressions is critical as well. The correct pronunciations of the Divine sounds have its positive effects on the heart and mind.

16. Allah ﷻ has mobile angels that only follow, attend, and are present in the circles and groups of worship, glorification and remembrance of Allah ﷻ. When they find such a group or circle, they sit with them. Then, they surround them with their wings until the space is filled between them the sky and the earth. When the people leave, the angels ascend and take off to the sky. Then, Allah ﷻ, the Exalted and the Glorious, although knows where they were, asks them: "Where are you coming from?" The angels reply: "we are coming from Your creation on the earth. They were praying, worshipping, and chanting to You through the phrases of perfection of Your Glory and removing all the wrong thoughts and feelings in their relationship with You, with a phrase of exalting Your Name, with a phrase of proclaiming Your Oneness, Uniqueness and Distinctiveness as the Creator, with an expression of expressing gratitude and appreciation for all Your bounties, and they are asking You. Allah ﷻ says: what are they asking from

Me? The angels say: "they ask Your Heaven." Allah ﷻ says: "did they see My Heaven?" The angels reply: "no, oh our Sustainer and Nourisher." Allah ﷻ says: what would happen if they saw My Heaven? Then, the angels continued "they ask protection." Allah ﷻ says: "from what do they ask protection?" The angels reply: "from Your fire, oh our Sustainer and Nourisher." Allah ﷻ says: what would happen if they saw My Fire?" Then, the angels continued "they ask Your forgiveness." Allah ﷻ says: "Indeed, I have forgiven them, I have given them what they ask for and protected them what they ask protection from." The angels continued "Oh our Sustainer and Nourisher! There was an unrelated person among them. This person was passing there and happened to sit with them." Allah ﷻ said: "I also forgave that person. This gathering and these people are such that whoever sits with them would be in no way unfortunate. [2] (2689)."

Commentary

The above narration is the full of version of the previous narration. It is split in two parts due to its length. As mentioned before, Allah ﷻ knows everything. Allah ﷻ makes angels witness everything as the creation of Allah ﷻ for the dealings of humans. At the same time, there is the occurrence of the Divine teaching method. There is an emphasis in the above testimony of Rasulullah ﷺ that Allah ﷻ appreciates a person's effort in their relationship with Allah ﷻ through prayers, remembrance and chants. In this perspective, the test and trial is about the belief in Allah ﷻ and all other unseen future encounters such as heaven, hell, and accountability of afterlife. When a person follows and submits oneself to the Divine guidelines of belief through the Quran and teachings of the Prophet Muhammad ﷺ although one may not fully see them, then Allah ﷻ assures that the person would get what he or she asks for.

In the last part of the above narration, there is the importance of being in good gatherings where Allah ﷻ is truly remembered and worshipped. A person may not feel fully in presence in these gatherings but with the intention of receiving Allah ﷻ's forgiveness, the person should still make an effort to be there. In other words, in Islam, it is very critical to choose good, God-conscious friends and environments in order to receive and benefit from the blessings bestowed by Allah ﷻ to individuals, gatherings and environments.

17. Abu Musa said: "we were on a journey with Rasulullah ﷺ. The people traveling with us were chanting "Allah ﷻ is Exalted and the Greatest" with a loud voice. Rasulullah ﷺ said to them: "Oh People! You are not calling the One Who is deaf and absent. Certainly, you are calling the One Who is All Hearing, Present and Close. Allah ﷻ is always with you [2] (2704).

Commentary

Sometimes our human renderings urge us to engage with Allah ﷻ in a similar way that we engage ourselves with people. When we don't see people with our eyes we tend to shout or increase our voice so that they can hear us. When a person does not respond to us in the way that we accept and assume then we assume that the person did not hear us. Then, we tend to repeat what we said and increase our voice. When we project exactly the same renderings with one's relationship with Allah ﷻ, it may have problems. In this case to eliminate these problematic projections in one's relationship with Allah ﷻ and humans, Rasulullah ﷺ reminds that Allah ﷻ is All Hearing, All Present and Close. Allah ﷻ is always with the person.

18. Oh my Sustainer and Nourisher, my God, forgive me my faults, forgive my ignorance in my relation with You, forgive my immoderations in all of my actions and my dealings with You and others. You already know all of them. Oh my Sustainer and Nourisher, my God, forgive me my faults that I committed in seriousness or otherwise, forgive my faults that I committed deliberately and knowingly. Yes, I admit, all these are mine. Oh my Sustainer and Nourisher, my God, forgive me my faults that I rushed into and I delayed, forgive me my faults that I committed in private and public. You already know all of them. You are the First and Last and You have the Full Power over anything and everything, [2] (2719).

Commentary

Above is a supplication of the Prophet Muhammad 🕊 that he teaches to Muslims to embody a relationship between Allah 🕊 as the Creator. In this case, the first disposition of the person is to accept and reveal everything to Allah 🕊 in one's internal and external dealings. This is a virtuous state. To be in this state, one should know oneself with self-reflection and accountability. Then, he or she can realize that there is a Being, Allah 🕊, Who knows all these renderings of a person truly and fully although the person does or does not realize it, or accepts it or not. Once the person admits this position then, the next step is conversing and talking with Allah 🕊 as the needy, faulty, weak creation or worshipper as used in Islam. This disposition in reality makes the person very powerful because the person is connected to the One Who is All and Full powerful. One can realize in the above supplication that there is a very genuine revealing of one's inner self in front of Allah 🕊.

19. Abu Zarr reported, Rasulullah 🕊 said to me" Should I inform you about the most liked words by Allah 🕊?", I said "Oh Messenger of God, please tell me the most liked words by Allah 🕊?" Rasulullah 🕊 then said: "the most liked words by Allah 🕊 is SubhanAllah wabi hamdihi, Allah 🕊 is Perfect, without any human misconstructions and wrong ideas about Allah 🕊, all true glory, praise, thanks and gratitude is due to Allah 🕊 [2] (2731R1).

Commentary

One of the frequent phrases chanted by Muslims is "SubhanAllah" and "Alhamdullilah." When this expression is combined then, one can say it as "SubhanAllah wabi hamdihi." It can be chanted as a separate or combined term. These two important phrases summarize the essence of religion in one's relationship with Allah 🕊. The first one is the true knowledge about Allah 🕊 as expressed with "SubhanAllah." The person removes all the negative feelings, ideas and constructions about Allah 🕊 with this phrase. Then, the next phrase is the attitude of grace, appreciation, respect and thankfulness towards Allah 🕊 with the expression of Alhamdulillah.

20. Allah ﷻ is happy and pleased with the repentance of a believing person similar to a traveler in a desert who loses his riding animal which has all his provisions, food, and drink. He falls asleep out of frustration. Then, he wakes up and goes everywhere to look for his ride until he becomes so tried, exhausted and thirsty. Then, he goes back fully exhausted where he was before, puts his head between his two hands so that he can fall asleep waiting for his death in this desert. Then, at one point, he opens eyes and lifts a little bit his head and sees right next to him his riding animal with all his provisions, food and drink. Indeed, and for sure, Allah ﷻ becomes more pleased with the repentance of a believing person than this man finding and recovery of his ride with all his provisions [2] (2744).

Commentary

Above testimony of Rasulullah ﷺ shows the importance of one's constant and personal relationship with Allah ﷻ in Islam. One can realize that Allah ﷻ wants humans to realize that the rope to establish connection with the Divine is always there through repentance. Repentance can be the disposition of a person, realizing his or her own mistakes in front of Allah ﷻ and asking forgiveness from Allah ﷻ with regret and sincerity. In Islam, the best person is the one who constantly repents to Allah ﷻ. It is part of human weakness and nature to make mistakes and sins. Rasulullah ﷺ says "all humans can make mistakes and sins yet, the best one among them is the person who always goes back to Allah ﷻ and asks for forgiveness [4] [5]."

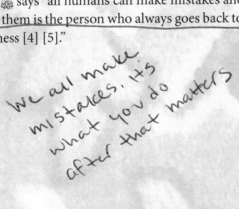
We all make mistakes, its what you do after that matters

21. Rasulullah 🌸 said "Allah 🌸 made mercy in <u>hundred parts</u>. Allah 🌸 retained the ninety-nine parts of it and <u>sent one part upon earth</u>. From this part is the <u>inherent love, mercy and caring</u> of the <u>creatures towards others</u>. Even, it is from this part of mercy, love and caring for an animal trying to carry their child with their hoof or horn with a fear of hurting them [2] (2752).

Commentary

One can realize from the above testimony of Rasulullah 🌸 that there are intrinsic and inherent qualities of humans given to them such as love, caring and mercy towards other creations. This intrinsic quality is also given by Allah 🌸. One should realize that Allah 🌸 is the Most Merciful and Most Caring. In other words, Allah 🌸 is more merciful than the person's mother or their loved ones as indicated in the statements of Rasulullah 🌸 [2] [6]. This notion is critical in Islam that when people question Allah 🌸's interference in evil-seeming incidents, the person is reminded that Allah 🌸 sees everything and Allah 🌸 is the Most Merciful and Most Caring and there is no comparison of Divine Mercy, Love and Caring of the Creator in both quality and quantity. The expression the Most Merciful and Most Caring translates as Ar-Rahman and Ar-Rahim which is repeated in the beginning of virtually each chapter in the Quran. In other words, <u>God or Allah in Islam introduces the Divine</u> <u>Self with mercy in the Quran in the beginning of each chapter except</u> one[6]. According to some interpretations sending one part on earth and retaining the ninety-nine parts can also mean that the retained parts of mercy, love and caring will be demonstrated in the afterlife immensely.

God keeps 99 + sends 1
— wants to be clear of the value to the reader

---

6. There are 114 chapters in the Quran. All start with the expression of "Bismillahi Rahmani Rahim" which translates as "in the Name of the Most Merciful and the Most Caring," except the 9th chapter.

22. Rasulullah ﷺ said "Allah ﷻ has all the love, mercy, compassion, and caring. Allah ﷻ sent one percent of this mercy, compassion, love and caring among humans, Jinn, the unseen beings, animals and insects. Therefore, they have the love, mercy, compassion and caring towards each other. Even, it is from this part of mercy, love, compassion, and caring for wild and predator animals treating their children and babies with mercy, love, compassion, and caring. Allah ﷻ retained ninety-nine percent of the Divine Mercy for the creation for the Day of Judgement [2] (2752R2).

Commentary

The above testimony is the same narration from Rasulullah ﷺ with slightly different wordings. In this narration, the love, caring, mercy and compassion of all animals and even insects towards each other is due to and from the Real Source, Allah ﷻ. It is interesting to note that the wild-seeming animals such as wolfs, lions, tigers even insects and snakes have mercy and compassion towards their children as mentioned in the above statement. This intrinsic quality in creation shows that all the creation has a purpose in life as well as the humans. In this narration, there is the explicit mention that Allah ﷻ would treat the creation with utmost mercy after their death in their accountability. Therefore, in Islam, the person does not really deserve to go Heaven with his good deeds but granted by Allah ﷻ as the projection of this Mercy on this person. In Islam, Allah ﷻ grants the Divine Mercy on the ones who believe and appreciate Allah ﷻ with humbleness and humility. In this regard, the attitude or intention is the key rather than the outcome or action.

w/which
even those we may not clearly see their mercy/love/compassion/caring

23. Umar reported that after a war, there was a woman among them in the field looking for someone. Then, she found a child and hugged and pressed the baby against her chest and let the baby suckle from her. Observing this incident, Rasulullah ﷺ said to us "Do you expect this lady throwing her baby in fire?" We said: "Definitely no! but she has the ability to do so." Then, Rasulullah ﷺ said: "Allah ﷻ is much more Merciful, Caring and have compassion to the creation than this lady has to her baby, [2] (2754).

Commentary

Above is an interesting and very descriptive narration from Rasulullah ﷺ. After a war, there is a chaotic environment of destruction. Everyone is looking for their lost and loved ones and here is a mother looking for her baby in a battle field. She is probably acting frantically, fearfully and desperately to find her baby in the field among others. After sometime of these panicking moments, she finally finds her baby and hugs and presses the baby against her chest with an enormous relief. At this time, watching this incident, Rasulullah ﷺ mentions that Allah ﷻ's Mercy and Caring is indeed much more on the creation and humans than this mother's towards her child.

reminder that humans will never truly understand even a mother/child who were seperated

24. Rasulullah ﷺ related from Allah ﷻ. A person committed a sin. Then, this person said: "Oh my Sustainer and Nourisher, Allah ﷻ, forgive my sins!" Then, Allah ﷻ, the Most Glorious and Exalted said "My worshipper committed a sin and was aware that this person had a Sustainer and Nourisher, Allah ﷻ Who forgives the sins but also has the ability and power of taking account of the sin." Later, this person went back and again committed a sin. Then, this person said: "Oh my Sustainer and Nourisher, God, forgive my sins!" Then, God, the Most Glorious and Exalted said "My worshipper committed a sin and was aware that this person had a Sustainer and Nourisher, God Who forgives the sins but also has

the ability and power of taking account of the sin!" Later again, this person went back and committed a sin. Then, this person said: "Oh my Sustainer and Nourisher, God, forgive my sins!" Then, God, the Most Glorious and Exalted said "My worshipper committed a sin and was aware that this person had a Sustainer and Nourisher, God Who forgives the sins but also has the ability and power of taking account of the sin." Then, Allah ﷻ said "do whatever you want, after this indeed I have granted forgiveness for you," [2] (2658).

Commentary

In Islam, the essence of the mystery of the creation is understanding who we are as humans. Namely, we make mistakes and we should recognize it. As humans, the person should recognize one's mistakes and ask forgiveness from people as needed but always from Allah ﷻ. The above narration underlines the importance of realizing that one has a Creator, Allah ﷻ. The person is accountable with all their actions in front of Allah ﷻ. After this step, it is critical to be honest and sincerely make a confession to Allah ﷻ at a personal and private account and ask forgiveness from Allah ﷻ. When the person makes this as a habit or as one's trait, then the person is in a virtuous condition in one's relationship with Allah ﷻ. Therefore, the last part of the above narration as "do whatever you want, after this indeed I have granted forgiveness for you" alludes to the notion that as long as the person makes a mistake and then goes back and ask forgiveness from Allah ﷻ, then Allah ﷻ would forgive him or her. One should realize in the above testimony that it is normal to make mistakes, sins, or errors as humans. What is abnormal and odd can be if one is heedless about it. In other words, Allah ﷻ appreciates the intention and the effort but not the outcome of the achievements or failures in Islamic creed. It is also related in many of the Islamic discourses that when a person is on a constant roll of mistakes, sins and assumes that Allah ﷻ would not forgive him or her, then this is considered as a deception and trapping instigated by Satan [7].

asking forgiveness as habit
✱ w/ intention

25. No one loves and accepts regrets and being asked for forgiveness like Allah ﷻ does. Therefore, Allah ﷻ has sent scriptures, divine books, messengers and prophets [2] (2760R3).

Commentary

This narration explains better the previous narration from Rasulullah ﷺ. A person may not truly realize the attributes of the Creator, Allah ﷻ. He or she may not realize what is expected in one's relationship with Allah ﷻ. Therefore, Allah ﷻ has sent scriptures, divine books, messengers and prophets to inform that there is only One Creator. One of the most important attributes of the Creator is that Allah ﷻ loves and accepts regrets and forgiveness from the creation. As mentioned before, when the person understands that it is normal to make mistakes and to sin, as humans are weak and in need. Yet, it is expected with one's relationship with Allah ﷻ to relentlessly and persistently go back, ask forgiveness and establish a positive relationship with Allah ﷻ. This does not mean that Allah ﷻ likes sins. Allah ﷻ likes the effort of the person after making a mistake or sin, going back to Allah ﷻ with regret and asking for forgiveness.

26. Allah ﷻ expects commitment and loyalty with gratitude from the person. A believer in Allah ﷻ also expects commitment and reliability with thankfulness in human relations. The commitment and loyalty between the person and Allah ﷻ is cracked and harmed when the person commits sins or actions disliked by Allah ﷻ [2] (2761).

Commentary

This testimony of Rasulullah ﷺ about Allah ﷻ is very critical to analyze in our contemporary time. A similar understanding is present in Christian and Jewish theology. Yet, due to problems, I believe, of the translations and human contextualizing, in these two sister theologies of Islam, the phrase that one often hears is a "jealous Allah ﷻ,". In Islam, referring to Allah ﷻ with this phrase can be considered as blasphemy. Because, jealousy is a negative quality in most human discourses and Allah ﷻ does not have any human negative qualities. Allah ﷻ is the source of all perfect and complete attributes and names manifested in the creation and in humans.

99 [(handwritten margin note)

The similar original word in Arabic in the above translation that is used and often mistranslated in its contexts has the meaning of commitment and loyalty. The same word in Arabic can also be used for the spousal relationships. When there is a relationship there is an expected commitment and loyalty between the partners. In this perspective, regardless of religious affiliation, it is very difficult to witness one's partner having a relationship with another person. In this context, this is not jealousy, maybe positive expectation of loyalty, trust, reliability, gratitude and commitment. Therefore, in the traditional historical stories, slave and master stories are exemplified to show this loyalty between the person and Allah ﷻ. Perhaps today, this can be best exemplified with partner relationships. When Allah ﷻ sends scriptures, divine books, messengers and prophets, there is the expectation of people following their guidelines. In this perspective, there is a commitment and trust between the person and Allah ﷻ about the person following these teachings. One can also call this as a covenant similar to the terms in Christian and Jewish theologies. This fidelity and devotion is harmed when the person breaks or harms this covenant by not following these divine guidelines. Yet, it is important to recognize from the previous narrations from the Prophet Muhammad ﷺ that asking forgiveness with regret can repair this weakened relationship between the person and Allah ﷻ.

Allah will grant forgiveness, but that doesn't mean nothing was broken (handwritten note)

27. In the past nations, there was a man who killed ninety-nine people. He regretted and wanted to repent. Then, he asked around to find out who was the most knowledgeable in religion that could help him. People directed him to a monk, a worshipper of Allah ﷻ. The man came to the monk and said: "Indeed, I killed ninety-

nine people. Is there any forgiveness for me from Allah ﷻ? The monk said: "no." Then, the man killed the monk. He completed his killings to hundred people. Again, he kept his search and asked around to find out who was the most knowledgeable in religion that could help him. The people directed him to a religious scholar. Then, the man went to the scholar and said: Indeed, I killed one-hundred people. Is there any forgiveness for me from Allah ﷻ? The scholar said: "yes, who can come between the forgiveness of Allah ﷻ and the person! Go to a new town in a different place than your hometown which I will direct you to. They worship Allah ﷻ, and, worship with them and stay there with them! Do not go to your old hometown. There is a lot of evil there." The man left. As he was almost in the middle of his way to reach his destination, the moment of death came to him, he turned his chest towards his destined city, pushed forward himself as much as he could and died. Then immediately on the scene, there was a dispute between the angels of mercy and angels of punishment. The angels of mercy said: "this man was seeking Allah ﷻ for repentance and asking forgiveness with a sincere, regretful and remorseful heart. The angels of punishment said:" he did not have any single good thing in his life." Then, another angel came on the scene in the form of a human and interfered in the dispute and said: "measure the distance between these two destinations, where ever place he is close to, then the man is theirs." They measured and found that the man was close to his destined city. Then, the angels of mercy took him, [2] (2766, & 2766R1).

Commentary

The above testimony of Rasulullah ﷺ alludes that there is always forgiveness from Allah ﷻ even the person committed major crimes, evils and sins. As long as the person recognizes their position that the person has an only one Creator, Allah ﷻ. In the above case, there is a serial killer who killed one hundred people but looking for forgiveness and repentance from Allah ﷻ. In some of the other versions of the above narration, before the angels measured the distance between two towns, Allah ﷻ contracted the earth to make the man nearer to his destination city so that angels of mercy could take the man with them. Another point in this narration is the importance of knowledge. When the man goes to the monk, a pious worshipper, the monk gives this man a wrong counsel. Then, when this man goes to a scholar, the scholar gives the man the correct counsel. In Islam, the true scholarship includes both piety and knowledge. Therefore, scholars are considered at a higher level than mere pious worshippers although both qualities of piety and knowledge is very paramount in Islam.

Moreover, the man's last posture and effort before his death mentioned above as "he turned his chest towards his destined city, pushed forward himself as much as he could." This signifies the man's discerning and expressive effort and struggle in his relationship with Allah ﷻ. In Islam, Allah ﷻ values the intentions and struggles but not misleading outcomes. In this perspective, the man's last push and throwing his body forward is very meaningful and insightful that he tries until his last breath to ask forgiveness from Allah ﷻ.

Another important point is the need for changing environment when a person wants to change oneself. The scholar specifically suggests the man to be with the people of Allah ﷻ. This stance can help a person to change easily. Sometimes, our willpower may not be strong to change although we want to change. Being in the flow of good people can also push the person to change in the direction of good when a person is with them.

Evil-Seeming Incidents & Destiny

Never is a believer touched by something evil, tragedy, hardship or illness, stress, anxiety or any mental or emotional worry that then, they become closer to Allah سبحانه وتعالى with this affliction which removes all past offenses [2] (2573).

1. Never is a believer touched by something evil, tragedy, hardship or illness, stress, anxiety or any mental or emotional worry then, they become closer to God with this affliction which removes all of their past offenses [2] (2573).

Commentary

According to the above testimony of Rasulullah ﷺ, the evil-seeming incidents are in their essence blessings from Allah سبحانه وتعالى. There are other narrations from Rasulullah ﷺ that mention that Allah سبحانه وتعالى gives tribulations to the one who Allah سبحانه وتعالى loves in order to elevate their spiritual status and they become closer to Allah سبحانه وتعالى. In this sense, it is a common practice that Muslims remind the people who are afflicted with something evil that Allah سبحانه وتعالى loves that person and it is a blessing for her or him. One should distinguish that one should not ask evil from Allah سبحانه وتعالى but always ask happiness in life and afterlife. When evil touches the person, the above testimony sets the spiritual and mindful disposition of the person that the person who is touched with evil should not complain but still be thankful to Allah سبحانه وتعالى. There is an understanding that the person meets with Allah سبحانه وتعالى when he or she dies in the state of utmost purity when all the past offenses are removed through tests, trials and evil-seeming incidents.

2. Nothing happens to a believer, even a tiny prick in one's body, or bigger than this, but that Allah سبحانه وتعالى elevates this person's status and level. Or, Allah سبحانه وتعالى forgives with this tribulation, all the past offenses and sins of this person [2] (2572R1).

Commentary

According to the above testimony of Rasulullah ﷺ, anything a person who believes in Allah سبحانه وتعالى faces in life as a difficulty or something evil-seeming is in reality a means to elevate the person in one's relationship with Allah سبحانه وتعالى. Allah سبحانه وتعالى gives this person immense rewards if the person is patient and appreciative of what he or she already has. Even if this is something minor as mentioned as a tiny prick in the above statement. This can change one's perspective when someone faces something evil instead of cursing or getting angry. Therefore, Muslims are expected to say "Alhamdulillah" which means "I am still thankful to Allah سبحانه وتعالى for whatever Allah سبحانه وتعالى gives me," whenever they face evil-looking incidents.

again, say w/ ♡ + lips?

3. In a long narration from Abu Zharr from Rasulullah ﷺ, Rasulullah ﷺ mentioned that Allah سبحانه وتعالى said[7]: "If a person finds good and blessings in one's life, the person should be thankful and grateful to Allah سبحانه وتعالى. If a person finds the opposite in one's life, the person should blame oneself [2] (2577).

contradiction of earlier?

be they aren't believing in Allah?

Commentary

In Islamic creed, all the blessings and good in its essence are given by Allah سبحانه وتعالى. The person can work for it. Allah سبحانه وتعالى enables the person to be in these blessings. Then, the person does not become arrogant or conceited about these blessings that he or she is in but thanks Allah سبحانه وتعالى for all of it. Oppositely, if the person finds them self in opposite looking incidents and encounters, the expected

---

7. Normal narrations or sayings of the Prophet Muhammad are called, Hadith. The types of narrations of the Prophet Muhammad from God are called special narrations, Hadith Qudsi.

attitude of a Muslim is to be patient. If he or she wants to look at a reason or a cause of this incident, one should make self-reflection and accountability of oneself. In these situations of evil, as mentioned in the previous statement of Rasulullah ﷺ, this evil-seeming encounter can in reality be the means to elevate the person in their relationship with Allah سبحانه وتعالى. Allah سبحانه وتعالى gives this person immense rewards if the person is patient and appreciative of what he or she has. In the concepts of evil or theodicy, the person is always expected to maintain positive, appreciative and graceful relationship with Allah سبحانه وتعالى.

---

4. Whoever dies not believing in destiny is not from me [1] (4700).

Commentary

Above is a part of longer narration from the Prophet Muhammad ﷺ. One of the important pillars in Islam is the belief in destiny. This makes the person not to extremely blame oneself or others when it becomes destructive. Self-blame or learning from the mistakes is a virtue as long as it is done in proportion but not in excess so that it doesn't become destructive. Therefore, when there are things that are out of one's control, then the notion of destiny is present itself. There are a lot of things in life that one cannot control. In the above narration, Rasulullah ﷺ mentions that one's belief is not complete unless they also believe, understand, and implement the notion of destiny in one's life.

---

5. One day, Rasulullah ﷺ was talking to some women from Ansar and he said: No three children of yours dies and you still keep patience except that you enter Heaven. Then, one woman from them asked: how about two children, oh Messenger of Allah سبحانه وتعالى؟ Rasulullah ﷺ said: Even two! [2] (2632R2).

Commentary

The above testimony of Rasulullah ﷺ shows how a trial or evil-seeming incident can be a means for a person to relieve one's pain and motivate the person be positive and patient. In this case, when a person loses one's children due to any type of death, Allah سبحانه وتعالى places this person in Heaven because of one's patience in difficult times of pain. As one can see that in Islam, life has trials, tests and difficulties. Allah سبحانه وتعالى rewards the people when they keep patience and their covenant with Allah سبحانه وتعالى in gratitude through prayers with constant appreciation in these times of difficulty and evil-seeming incidents.

again, performative? genuine?

6. One day, Abu Hasan came to Abu Huraira and said: my two children died. Do you know anything from Rasulullah ﷺ that would calm our heart due our loss? Abu Huraira said: yes. Rasulullah ﷺ said: The small children are similar to the birds of Heaven. The child will hold from his or her parents' clothes and hands so tightly until Allah سبحانه وتعالى gives permission for the parents to enter Heaven [2] (2635).

Commentary

In the above narration, if children die at a young age they enter immediately to Heaven. There is no accountability for children compared to adults when they die. Then, these children beg pardon and insist to Allah سبحانه وتعالى until they get permission to take their parents to Heaven. One can see that it is a very difficult situation for parents who lost their children. When they know that their children are in Heaven and they will be means for them to go to Heaven, it can give them some solace for their pain and loss.

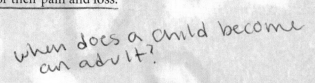

when does a child become an adult?

7. One day a woman came to Rasulullah ﷺ holding her child and said: Oh Messenger of Allah! Please pray for this child! I already lost my previous three children and buried them. Rasulullah ﷺ said: You already buried three of your children? She said: yes. Rasulullah ﷺ said: Indeed, you protected yourself with a very strong shield against the punishment of hellfire [2] (2636).

Commentary

Above narration shows that every evil-seeming incident has a meaning and a positive outcome for the person if the person keeps patience and an appreciative relationship with Allah سبحانه وتعالى. Rasulullah ﷺ emphasizes in the above narration that Allah سبحانه وتعالى will recompense and reward her pain in the afterlife. In Islam, Allah سبحانه وتعالى tests people in this world with ugly-seeming incidents to reward them and elevate their status. If one can review the friends of Allah سبحانه وتعالى in Islam, they had very difficult lives externally, but they were in happiness and joy internally and did not complain but were always appreciative with gratitude in their relationship with Allah سبحانه وتعالى.

8. Rasulullah ﷺ narrated that Allah سبحانه وتعالى said "I am close to My servant's thoughts about what he or she thinks about Me [2] (2675)."

Commentary

Above is the announcement of Allah سبحانه وتعالى about the importance of one's positive and good assumptions about Allah سبحانه وتعالى. Especially, in the renderings of theodicy, if a person is always in a blame mode to Allah سبحانه وتعالى for the encounters of evil, it cannot be a good assumption but unfruitful disposition for the person. Therefore, a person in Islam is always required to have a good opinion, assumption and expectation about Allah سبحانه وتعالى in this world and afterlife. Then, Allah سبحانه وتعالى treats the person according to this person's good, positive and constructive relationship, feelings and thoughts about Allah سبحانه وتعالى. However, if the person is always in a blame mode and expects nothing after death, then the person can possibly end up in a situation that Allah سبحانه وتعالى may treat this person according to what he or she portrays in their mind and heart.

so Allah knows intention (28)

9. Rasulullah ﷺ narrated that Allah سبحانه وتعالى said "I am close to My servant's thoughts about what he or she thinks about Me. I am with this person when he or she calls Me. If one calls Me in oneself, then I call him or her in Myself. If one glorifies Me in a gathering then, I honor this person in a much better gathering. If one comes close to Me a hand's distance, I come close this person an arm's distance. If one comes close to Me a foot's distance, I come close to this person a mile distance. If one comes close to Me walking, I come close to this person running [2] (2675)."

Commentary

Above is the continuation of the previous narration which has a clear metaphorical and figurative language. The essence of the above narration explains that when a person makes an effort of establishing relationship with Allah سبحانه وتعالى, Allah سبحانه وتعالى appreciates that and makes it easy for this person. Allah سبحانه وتعالى is above and beyond from human renderings of distance, walking, or running. In the Quran and sayings of Rasulullah ﷺ, sometimes there is metaphorical language to make the people understand a message easy and personalize it in one's relationship with Allah سبحانه وتعالى. In the encounters of theodicy or evil, one can understand from above narration that Allah سبحانه وتعالى always appreciates and responds to human's genuine efforts to establish relationship with their Creator. Therefore, Allah سبحانه وتعالى is always Present, Alive, Active, Interfering and Forgiving.

10. None of you should desire death due to hardship that falls on a person. If one cannot help it, then he or she should say: "oh Allah! Keep me alive as long as there is goodness in life for me and bring death to me when there is goodness in death for me [2] (2680).

Commentary

In Islam, one of the grave sins is to kill oneself or commit suicide. No one has the right to end one's life except God. This time is unknown to each individual to the Divine Wisdom. A person should make all the efforts to live long. If there are times when a person cannot handle the difficulties in life, then the person should still not ask death from God. However, if it comes to an unbearable point, then the person can pray and ask from God as in the above testimony of Rasulullah.

11. None of you should wish to die. Do not ask and pray for death before it comes. When one of you dies, the good deeds of the person stop. The life a believer who has appreciation and gratitude for God is not prolonged except there is goodness in it [2] (2782).

Commentary

Above is a similar narration as the previous one. A person who has a positive, appreciative and grateful relationship with God should not desire and ask God for death. When the person is alive and does good actions, this person increases his or her good deeds before the accountability after death. With this intention, one can seek all the means to live longer as mentioned by Rasulullah.

12. Abu Hazim said that one day, I visited Habbab who had seven
    holes on his belly due to the torture of fire burnt on his skin. He
    said to me: At the time, if the Messenger of God did not prohibit us
    from asking God for death, certainly I would have prayed to God
    for it [2] (2681).

Commentary

Above is a narration from the early Muslims with Rasulullah ﷺ. As one
can see, early Muslims were tortured and killed due to accepting Islam.
Habbab, a black Muslim who was with Rasulullah ﷺ tortured cruelly
due to his belief in one God. Still, Rasulullah ﷺ instructed them not
to pray and ask for death but be patient with the oppression and evil
renderings of people.

13. Oh Allah! I take refuge in You from incapacity, impairment,
    disability, laziness, weakness, being fearful, lack of courage, the
    weakness of old age, being stingy and I take refuge in You from
    the sufferings of grave, from the trials of life and death [2] (2706).

Commentary

Above is a widely practiced supplication of Rasulullah ﷺ among
Muslims. Rasulullah ﷺ teaches how to prevent some evil-seeming
incidents in one's life with prayer. When there are incidents that the
person has no control, human weakness reveals itself in its full capacity.
At these times, if the person does not take refuge in Allah سبحانه وتعالى
and ask help then, these evil-seeming incidents can destroy the person's
stamina. On the other hand, when the person knows that there is a
Being Who can help with all these uncontrolled incidents, the person
has ease in life.

14. Abu Huraira said Rasulullah ﷺ used to take refuge in Allah سبحانه وتعالى from the evil of destiny and evil outcomes, from falling in a calamity and hardship, from the mockery of enemies and adversaries and from the hardship of misery [2] (2707)

Commentary

Similar to the previous narration, Rasulullah ﷺ teaches how to prevent some evil-seeming incidents in one's life with prayer. It is important to constantly ask Allah سبحانه وتعالى protection from the unknown incidents of future.

15. A man came to Rasulullah ﷺ and said: "Oh Messenger of Allah!, I was stung by a scorpion yesterday night." Rasulullah ﷺ said: "when it became night if you said "I take refuge in the full, complete, comprehensive, and perfect words of Allah سبحانه وتعالى from the evil and harm of what Allah سبحانه وتعالى created", then nothing would have harmed you," [2] (2709).

Commentary

According to the above testimony of Rasulullah ﷺ, it is important for a person to take a position against all the unexpected evils in one's life. This is mainly performed by supplication and praying. Rasulullah ﷺ in this case shows the antidote curing words to protect oneself. This alludes to the importance of knowledge and learning in Islam to cope accordingly against the difficulties of life and prepare oneself for afterlife. The above wordings of Rasulullah ﷺ are one of the widely practiced litanies among the Muslims to protect oneself against all evil renderings. Rasulullah ﷺ suggests that Muslims should read this prayer at least twice immediately at night and in the morning.

In this hadith, one can try to understand what "I take refuge in the full, complete, comprehensive, and perfect words of Allah سبحانه وتعالى from the evils and harms of what Allah سبحانه وتعالى created" mean. As the person is weak, and there are seen and unseen evil beings, it is impossible to protect oneself physically and spiritually from all these evils and harms. When the person understands this weakness with humbleness and humility in their mind and heart, then they can take an immediate refuge in Allah سبحانه وتعالى for protection. The practical way of taking refuge in Allah سبحانه وتعالى is by verbalizing the disposition of heart and mind that the person submits oneself to Allah سبحانه وتعالى, the Creator of everything.

In Islam, the best way to verbalize it is to embody these meaning of refuge, submission and humility for Allah سبحانه وتعالى as taught to us by Allah سبحانه وتعالى in the Quran and through the teachings of Rasulullah ﷺ. With all these perspectives, if one says constantly this prayer in the morning and at night as "I take refuge in the full, complete, comprehensive, and perfect words of Allah سبحانه وتعالى from the evil and harm of what Allah سبحانه وتعالى created," then this person becomes untouchable and protected from all evils and harms according to the testimony of Rasulullah ﷺ.

---

16. Oh Allah!, I take refuge in You from the evils that I did and I take refuge in You from the evils that I did not do [2] (2716).

Commentary

According to a lot of scholars, the gist and essence of religion and Islam is the etiquette and respect[8] towards Allah سبحانه وتعالى. It is not really a calculation system of do's and don'ts and the reward and punishment system similar to an accountant agency although it motivates a lot of people and it has a value. Yet, it is one's inner disposition and attitude of heart and mind in their relationship with Allah سبحانه وتعالى. Can the person have always good, positive and appreciative feelings towards Allah سبحانه وتعالى? Or, is it always the human nature of blaming, stingy, ungrateful and unappreciative attitude? In this regard, although Rasulullah ﷺ as an exceptional human is protected by Allah سبحانه وتعالى from all the evil renderings, he still asks forgiveness for the present, past and future evil renderings. According to the scholars [8], this is why

---

8. adab

he is considered as the highest human who Allah سبحانه وتعالى created in history. Rasulullah ﷺ also does it, so that the followers can imitate him in this essential attitude of oneself with Allah سبحانه وتعالى. Then, the etiquette and respect for all the creation can follow as a natural disposition in a person due to the embodied respect to the Creator. On another interpretation, a person can maintain a true humbleness and humility when the person considers their valuable and pious actions as a possible source of evil such as arrogance. In this sense as the above testimony of Rasulullah ﷺ states, asking protection and refuge in Allah سبحانه وتعالى from all past and future and known and unknown renderings can be truly uplifting for the person in front of Allah سبحانه وتعالى. In addition, the expression "I take refuge in You from the evils that I did not do" can refer to the things the person did not do, but because the others may have some spiritual problems they may assume and think bad and evil about this person and possibly cause problems. For example, in a normal day, a person can be preoccupied with something and may not realize another person's greeting. The greeter can possibly assume something bad about this person. Then, the evil occurrence can possibly start.

17. Ibn Abbas reported that Rasulullah ﷺ used to make the supplication as: "Oh my God! I surrendered for You and to You, I believed in You, I relied on You, I turned to You, and I struggle and fight against the evil with Your help [2] (2717).

Commentary

Above is a testimony of Rasulullah ﷺ of how one's disposition should be in the encounters of life. First, the person is always in need and weak. As the person gets old or especially afflicted with sickness or tribulations, the reality of human weakness reveals itself without any blurring or background noise from the human ego. Although the word "surrender" in the above case may have some negative connotations in our contemporary time and bother some people, one should think of the practical implications of the notion of surrender in our daily affairs. The Prophetic suggestions in the above testimony have two possibilities

from the translation of the original language. First, the preposition is
"for" as "I surrendered for You" which can mean that my ego did not
want to surrender and submit but I did it for Your sake and pleasure.
The second possible proposition is "to" as "I surrendered to You" which
can mean that "I did not surrender and reveal my weakness as a human
to anyone else but except to You."

After this initial position, the real belief in Allah سبحانه وتعالى follows.
In this case, the action and attitude of submission and surrender comes
first before the verbal realization of the belief. After this attitude and
informed decision, the person relies on Allah سبحانه وتعالى in all good
and bad seeming incidents and turns regularly to Allah سبحانه وتعالى with
gratitude, and asks repentance and forgiveness from Allah سبحانه وتعالى.
Once the person passes these stages then he or she is ready to handle the
struggles and evil-seeming incidents in their life with the help of Allah
سبحانه وتعالى.

18. Ibn Abbas reported that the Prophet used to make the supplication
as: "Oh my Sustainer and Nourisher, I surrendered for You and
to You, I believed in You, I relied on You, I turned to You, and I
struggle and fight against the evil with Your help. Oh my Sustainer
and Nourisher, I take refuge in Your Greatness, there is no deity,
nothing but You, don't let me wander without Your Guidance, You
are the Always Present and Permanent Who doesn't die, yet all the,
jinn, invisible beings[9], and humans die, [2] (2717).

Commentary

Above is the continuation of the prior testimony of Rasulullah ﷺ.
Rasulullah ﷺ teaches the rational and embodiment of why a person
should turn to Allah سبحانه وتعالى for their needs. The main reason is that
all the creation, visible and invisible, humans and others have the same
need and fear of death and weakness. How can one help truly the other
if the person is in the same situation? In this regard, the person seeks
naturally the One Who doesn't die and always present.

---

9. jinn

19. Rasulullah ﷺ used to say at night: "Oh my Sustainer and Nourisher, my God! I ask the good of this night and the good that comes after it and follows, and I take refuge in You from the evil of this night and the evil that comes after and follows it." Rasulullah ﷺ used to say in the morning: "Oh my Sustainer and Nourisher, my God! I ask the good of this day and the good that comes after it and follows, and I take refuge in You from the evil of this day and the evil that comes after and follows it" [2] (2723R1).

Commentary

Rasulullah ﷺ teaches that each new night and day can carry good and evil. When the person supplicates to Allah سبحانه وتعالى in the beginning of each new day and night, then the person takes a deliberate stance for asking good and protection from the evil from Allah سبحانه وتعالى. In this perspective, there is assurance of Rasulullah ﷺ that when the person takes refuge in Allah سبحانه وتعالى and asks for good from Allah سبحانه وتعالى, the person's request would be indeed fulfilled. This is an example in Islam about the concept of reliance on Allah سبحانه وتعالى called tawakkul with supplication. The person can then feel off from one's burden. Another way of fulfilling the supplication is through taking measures for asking good and protection from evil. For example, in Islam should lock one's door at night and then ask Allah سبحانه وتعالى for protection. The person is considered to fulfill both active and verbal measures of fulfilling one's responsibility. After this stage, the state of the heart and mind of the person is called in reliance or tawakkul.

20. Ali reported that Rasulullah ﷺ said to him to say: "Oh my Sustainer and Nourisher, my God, guide me to the correct path and make me hold tightly with full correctness to it." Then, Rasulullah ﷺ added: "When you think about guidance think about a path or a road. When you think about staying firm on this path, think about the straightness of an arrow about to be thrown, [2] (2725).

Commentary

Above is the testimony of Rasulullah ﷺ how Muslims refer to correct path in their religious terminology as to be "on the straight path." One can see this in many of the English translations of the Quran especially in the translation of the first chapter. The above statement can allude to two ideal states in one's life. The first one is to choose the most correct and shortest path in order to please Allah سبحانه وتعالى in one's life. As there are a lot of religions, beliefs and engagements in one's spiritual life, the above teaching suggests that there is a path in the struggles of spiritual life which is the most pleasing to Allah سبحانه وتعالى. This path is the shortest, the most correct and the safest. The second part of the above statement implies possibly the difficulty of being regular following the straight path but yet, still asking the state of always adhering to this correct and shortest straight path in religious life. This supplication is very critical in a Muslim's life. Muslims are expected at least repeat this expression in five daily prayers at different times of day at a minimum of 20 times. Rasulullah ﷺ repeated this expression in his prayers at least 30 times daily with the optional prayers. All other possible paths can have different types of problems that could lead the person to some evil outcomes. Therefore, it is expected that when the person is on an ideal path of religious practice, the evil renderings can and should be minimized.

21. Everyone's prayer is answered as long as the person is not impatient and says "I have been praying for a long time and my prayer is not answered, or my prayer is not granted [2] (2735).

Commentary

Above is a testimony of Rasulullah ﷺ about a case that one can encounter often in one's life. Especially, the above statements of the person can reveal itself much at the encounters of evil. First, one should know that everyone's prayers and supplications are answered and granted by Allah سبحانه وتعالى. Either the person can understand or not, Allah سبحانه وتعالى gives the people what they ask or better for their desires achieving something beneficial. Sometimes the person understands it, and sometimes not. If it is not given at the desired time frame for the person, then there can be a time and place better than that Allah سبحانه وتعالى would give it to the person. In Islam, the life span includes both before and after death. In some cases, some of the things that the person asks would be granted to the person in one's life after death.

22. Oh Allah!, I take refuge in You from the loss of Your blessings, I take refuge in You from the change of my good conditions to bad conditions, I take refuge in You from any of Your immediate trials, punishments and tests, I take refuge in You from anything displeasing You [2] (2739).

Commentary

Above is a testimony of Rasulullah ﷺ that the person should constantly ask: easy, good and nice life from Allah ﷻ. One should not ask Allah ﷻ for trials or tests in order to show his or her strength of patience in their relationship with Allah ﷻ. Humans are weak and they can lose the tests in small challenges. However, if there is an evil-seeming incident that a person faces in one's life, then he or she should strength from Allah ﷻ to be patient and to maintain the of gratefulness and thanks to Allah ﷻ. In the above staten realize that in all the trials and tests one should run back spiritually to Allah ﷻ even if it is given by Allah ﷻ. There is none to take refuge in except Allah ﷻ. The scholars generally give the example of a mother with her children in this relationship. When the children are in trouble and the mother gets angry, the children still run back to the mother. This makes mother forgive their misbehavior.

23. The prayer of a person is answered and granted as long as the person does not pray for something evil, sin, cutting kinship relations or the person does not become impatient for the results of the prayer. Then, it was asked to Rasulullah ﷺ "how can a person be impatient, oh messenger of Allah ﷻ?" Rasulullah ﷺ said: "if he or she says, I prayed and prayed but I didn't see any signs that it was answered or accepted for me." Then, this person becomes doubtful and frustrated and stops praying, [2] (2735R2).

Commentary

One can realize from the above testimony of Rasulullah ﷺ that one's prayers are accepted and answered by Allah ﷻ as long as the person does not pray for something evil such as asking difficulty for a person, destruction of others, or distancing oneself from family members. A person should fully trust in Allah ﷻ that Allah ﷻ knows everyone's prayers, listens, and answers all the prayers as long as the person does not change their disposition in their full and firm trust in Allah ﷻ. Once the person becomes distrustful and stops praying then, this can be the possibility of one's prayer not being answered.

24. Rasulullah said "Allah made mercy in hundred parts. Allah retained the ninety-nine parts of it and sent one part upon earth. From this part is the inherent love, mercy and caring of the creatures towards others. Even, it is from this part of mercy, love and caring for an animal trying to carry their child with their hoof or horn with a fear of hurting them [2] (2752).

Commentary

One can realize from the above testimony of Rasulullah that there are intrinsic and inherent qualities of humans given to them such as love, caring and mercy towards other creations. This intrinsic quality is also given by Allah . One should realize that Allah is the Most Merciful and Most Caring. In other words, Allah is more merciful than the person's mother or their loved ones as indicated in the statements of Rasulullah [6] [2]. This notion is critical in Islam that when people question Allah 's interference in evil-seeming incidents, the person is reminded that Allah sees everything and Allah is the Most Merciful and Most Caring and there is no comparison of Divine Mercy, Love and Caring of the Creator with the creation in both quality and quantity. The expression the Most Merciful and Most Caring translates as Ar-Rahman and Ar-Rahim which is repeated in the beginning of each chapter in the Quran. In other words, Allah or Allah in Islam introduces the Divine Self with mercy in the Quran in the beginning of each chapter except one. According to some interpretations, sending one part on earth and retaining the ninety-nine parts can mean that the retained parts of mercy, love and caring will be demonstrated in the afterlife immensely.

Prayer

The separator between the belief and disbelief is the regular daily prayers [5] [2] [6] [3].

1. Rasulullah ﷺ said: "If there is a river in front of one's house and this person dives into this river five times a day, and takes a shower in it, do you think this person will be unclean?" The listeners around Rasulullah ﷺ replied "no." Rasulullah ﷺ then said: "Praying five times a day is similar. It wipes out and cleans all the mistakes and errors of the person." [6] [4] [9] [10] [2]

Commentary

Rasulullah ﷺ gives the example that a person praying five times a day cleans one's mistakes and sins from one prayer interval to the next one. The scholars mention that these mistakes are not the major ones but the minor ones. Major sins may need a different type of penitence.

2. The separator between the belief and disbelief is the five daily prayers. [2] [4] [1] [9]

Commentary

Five times daily prayer solidifies and maintains one's relationship with Allah ﷻ. It is normal to have cycles of stress and happiness during the day. Five times prayer balances one's spiritual, psychological and emotional mood, stamina and stability. There are a lot of newcomers to Islam in Western societies. One of the teachings that these newcomers find very valuable is the five-time prayers. John from New York, in one of the interviews says that, "it is amazing that you are required to unplug during the day and night with all these stresses to discharge yourself." [11]

3. Praying in the beginning of the time is the pleasure of Allah ﷻ. Praying in the last portion is the forgiveness of Allah ﷻ [12]:

Commentary

There is a time interval for each prayer that is performed five times a day. Each prayer can take a few minutes to pray. Depending on the prayer, a prayer interval can be from one and half hours to more than ten hours. According to this hadith, it is more rewarding to pray in the beginning of each prayer period although one can pray before the time ends to fulfill the requirement.

4. The Prophet Muhammad was asked about the best of the actions and he replied as the prayer performed at the beginning of its time. [1] [10] [4]

Commentary

It is the practice and advice of Rasulullah ﷺ that to perform prayers in the beginning of their time interval. Rasulullah ﷺ has other sayings about not delaying any good deed and doing immediately in case the person may not have the means to do it.

5. Rasulullah ﷺ used to delay the prayer within its time interval if it was too hot and he used to pray immediately as the time started when it was cold. [9]

Commentary

Rasulullah ﷺ used to always adapt easiness for the people. He used to emphasize this practice of easiness to the ones who were in the position of authority. A person can be demanding on her or himself in regards to the high levels of piety but he or she should always observe easiness with others.

6. Whoever prays in two cool times of the day regularly, then this
   person enters to Heaven. [6] [2]

Commentary

This saying of Rasulullah ﷺ about the two important prayer times, are
the morning (fajr) and late afternoon (asr) prayers. There is a special
emphasis not to miss these prayers. In some of the interpretations, this
can be due to difficulties of disturbance in sleeping in the morning and
the disturbance from working in the rush hour of the late afternoon. If
the person takes a few minutes of his or her time to pray, then there is
the reward of Heaven due to this self-struggle for the sake of Allah ﷻ.

7. Satan runs miles away, so far away to the place of Ravha when one
   sings the prayer call[10]. [2]

Commentary

It is the practice and suggestion of Rasulullah ﷺ that one should call and
sing the prayer call before starting the prayer. Satan hates and dislikes
the person's connection with Allah ﷻ through prayer. Therefore, as soon
as the prayer call is performed all the evil beings and Satan leave that
place, home and venue. The prayer calls are performed in loud speakers
five times a day outside the mosques in Muslim countries. In these
countries, it is interesting to observe during the prayer calls that dogs
especially bark. Some of the scholars interpret that unlike humans, dogs
see the running of the evil spirits and Satan therefore they bark.

8. Rasulullah ﷺ mentioned from Allah ﷻ about a shepherd with whom Allah ﷻ is much pleased: "Look at My Servant who makes the prayer call in the mountains and prays in solitude, with no one around, only doing for My Love and Fear. Definitely and certainly, I forgave My servant and placed this person in Heaven. [1]

Commentary

Calling to prayer is an important practice of Rasulullah ﷺ even though there may not be anyone to come and attend to the prayer around this person. The animals, the plants and all other beings recognize this person and all the evil spirits leaves that space. The remaining part of the saying of Rasulullah ﷺ emphasizes the sincerity of the person in one's relationship with Allah ﷻ. No one sees this person performing the prayer except this person has the intention of purely fulfilling the appreciation of Allah ﷻ.

9. Rasulullah ﷺ entered to Kabah with some of the disciples such as Bilal, Usama B. Zayd, and Osman B. Talha and stayed inside the Kabah for a while. When they came out, Bilal was asked what they did inside and he replied: "Rasulullah ﷺ prayed inside the Kabah." [6] [2]

Commentary

The Kabah is a cubicle structure believed to be built by the Prophet Abraham. It is currently located in Mecca, Saudi Arabia. Muslims turn towards Kabah during their prayer and they do pilgrimage to visit the Kabah. As one can see, the Kabah itself is one of the first temples built in human history to worship One God according to Muslims. Therefore, it is important to note for unfamiliar people that Muslims don't worship the Kabah but turn towards it while praying as a method of respect and recognition of this first temple of Allah ﷻ.

10. Rasulullah ﷺ was gazing at the Kabah and said: How valuable, nice and charming you are! But, for Allah ﷻ, the value of a believer is more than yours! [4]

Commentary

The value and holiness of the Kabah is very high in Islam. Rasulullah ﷺ reminds us that it is just a structure designated by Allah ﷻ to be respected. In reality, Allah ﷻ values a believer's genuine relationship with Allah ﷻ more than the Kabah. The saying of Rasulullah ﷺ instructs Muslims to prevent any type of idol worshipping with extreme respect to a material entity. The teachings of Islam sets boundaries to always worship One and only Allah ﷻ. Everything else is all creations, not the Creator even though they are sanctified.

11. The person who gets a lot of reward from Allah ﷻ is the one who goes to a masjid and mosque to pray from his house while his house is located in a far distance. Another person who is much appreciated by Allah ﷻ is the one who waits for the next prayer to pray in congregation compared to the one who prays by himself and sleeps. [6]

Commentary

The above hadith explains that Allah ﷻ puts value on the effort of the person when he or she has more difficulty than others. Islam teaches God consciousness in all parts of the day by praying, going to the mosque and mentally being in the state of awareness by awaiting the start of the next prayer. Therefore, it is not unusual for a Muslim to drive to the mosque a few times a day to pray with others although the prayer may only last a few minutes.

12. Pray some of your prayers at your homes. Do not turn your homes into graves by not praying in them [6] [2].

Commentary

It is important to pray especially the optional[11] prayers at home. The livelihood of a residence is established by the prayers inside. The angelic beings occupy this residence through angelic efforts of genuine prayers, and worship for Allah ﷻ. Therefore, it is important to greet when a person enters to his or her home by saying "assalumu alaykum" (peace upon you). In Islam, it is disliked to pray in the graves due to the wrong possible inclinations as if the person is worshipping death.

13. Be aware that the people of God habitually made the graves of their prophets and saints as their temples. Be careful! Do not take the graves of your pious ones as temples. I am discouraging you from this habit [2].

Commentary

One of the reasons of change of pure worship of Allah ﷻ is due to the extreme reverence of the saints or prophets viewed as divine. The above narration discourages worshipping and expecting benefit from the people who were dead. The only reality is to pray to Allah ﷻ, to only pray and ask help from God. Therefore, Rasulullah ﷺ deters Muslims from this practice in order them not to fall into a similar mistake of the previous nations.

---

11. Sunnah or Nawafil

14. It is a sign of the End of Days that people start boasting about the mosques, temples that they build [1].

Commentary

The purpose of a mosque is to genuinely, sincerely and purely worship Allah سبحانه وتعالى. It is permissible to build beautiful and nice masjids or mosques. Beautification of the mosques is secondary compared to the real purpose. If people lose the primary purpose and the architecture, ornaments, and decorations of the building becomes the main reason of visiting a mosque then it becomes an issue. In Islam, there is no theological requirement of beautifying the mosques, but there is a requirement of establishing venues for the people to get together and pray.

15. Rasulullah ﷺ did not sleep before praying the last prayer[12] and he did not engage in conversations after praying the last prayer. [6] [2]

Commentary

Rasulullah ﷺ did not sleep until he had prayed the last prayer. One of the recommendations of Rasulullah ﷺ by practice is not to involve oneself in conversations or in any engagement after the last prayer. There can be possible reasons for this advice:

▶ A person's last engagement should be praying before going to sleep because in Islam, sleeping is viewed as similar to death. Therefore, if the person dies while sleeping the last action of this person would be prayer when he or she meets with Allah سبحانه وتعالى.

▶ Waking up for the next prayer on time by sleeping immediately after the last prayer.

---

12. Isha

▶ Being efficient by waking up early for the next day by sleeping immediately after the last prayer.

▶ The possibilities of engaging in evil stipulations due to human hormonal changes and existence of other unseen beings released on earth at night time as Rasulullah ﷺ mentions in his other sayings.

---

16. The good dreams are from Allah سبحانه وتعالى and the bad dreams are from Satan. If one sees a dream that he or she is not pleased with, then one should spit on the left side and take refuge in Allah سبحانه وتعالى from Satan. This dream will not harm this person. Also, this person should not tell about this dream to any other person. If a person sees a good dream, then one should feel happy and pleased. She or he should not tell about this dream to any other person except the one who sincerely loves and wants always good for this person.

Commentary

Islam teaches how to deal with everyday encounters through prayers. It derives meanings for this life and the afterlife. If a person implements these teachings he or she can acquire positive results in this world and can receive rewards from Allah سبحانه وتعالى due to following the teachings of Rasulullah ﷺ and the Quran. In the above saying of Rasulullah ﷺ, a person who sees a bad dream can eliminate the disturbances of it by saying the phrase of protection[13] and by blowing on one's left side after waking up. He or she should not tell this dream to any other person but forget about it and move on. In the case of a good dream, it is important to recognize about it and be happy. The dreamer can share his or her dream with a trustworthy person who really looks always for the best interest of the dreamer.

---

13. Tawfiz: Eu'zu billahi min asshaytani rajim in Arabic.

17. When you visit the gardens of Heaven in this world then benefit from their fruits. Then, Rasulullah ﷺ was asked: "Oh Prophet of Allah What are the gardens of Heaven in this world?" Then, Rasulullah ﷺ replied: "The mosques and masjids where genuinely, truly and sincerely Allah سبحانه وتعالى is worshipped." Then, Rasulullah ﷺ was asked again: "What are their fruits?" Then, Rasulullah ﷺ replied: "by worshipping and chanting with:

► SubhanAllah: Exalted, Glorified and Free is Allah سبحانه وتعالى from all imperfections.

► Alhamdulillah: All appreciation, all praise and all thanks truly belongs to Allah سبحانه وتعالى.

► La ilaha illa Allah: There is no deity, and real power except Allah سبحانه وتعالى

► Allahu Akbar: Allah سبحانه وتعالى is Exalted, the Greatest and the Superior" [4] (83-3509)

Commentary

Any place that Allah سبحانه وتعالى is genuinely remembered is sacred and blessed. These places are often visited with unseen beings such as angels and other beings to bring tranquility, calmness and peace in the hearts of people. Therefore, a person who visits these places can feel the type of change in one's spiritual state. One of the places that is only dedicated to genuinely worship, pray, and chant for Allah سبحانه وتعالى is a mosque in Islam. There are a lot of theological rulings to protect the sole purpose of the temple, mosque in Islam. For example, one cannot do business transactions in mosques. One cannot shout. One cannot take impurities inside mosques. Therefore, if a person visits a mosque and sits in silence with reflection and waiting for a prayer then this action can be a worship by itself. If a person sits and chants the above four phrases mentioned by Rasulullah ﷺ, then he or she can benefit with a spiritual intake of positive feelings and rewards both in this world and afterlife. The above four phrases are the essence of the religious prayer rituals.

18. One day a desert man came to Rasulullah ﷺ and said "show me an action that if I do it I can go to Heaven." Then Rasulullah ﷺ replied as "believe and worship only one God without any associations, pray your five daily prayers, give charity to the poor and fast in the month of Ramadan." The man said "I swear, I will only do those, nothing more." After the man left Rasulullah ﷺ said "if someone wants to see a man of Heaven then one can look at this person [2] (38)."

Commentary

Islam sets the clear expectations for a person in order to fulfill one's obligations in this world for afterlife. In the above narration, the desert man is a simple uncomplicated individual. He does not want to follow the requirements of the religion except what is minimum. He asks accordingly and Rasulullah ﷺ answers it. The man affirms that he would do all the conditions without increasing or decreasing them. Rasulullah ﷺ finds his affirmation sincere. Rasulullah ﷺ realizes in his teachings that everyone is at a different level. He accordingly individualizes his instruction for the teachings of the religion. One of the principles that Rasulullah ﷺ urges people to implement in teaching the religion is that making the rules and practices of the religion easy for people.

19. One day, Rasulullah ﷺ was praying and there was a type of curtain with distracting bright colors and shapes in front of him. Rasulullah ﷺ asked his wife, saying: "could you remove the curtain while I am praying? Because its shapes and colors distract my concentration during the prayer" [6] (Salah 15).

Commentary

It is important to fully concentrate in meditation and prayers. Therefore, Rasulullah ﷺ advises to choose places and prayer areas with less and minimal distractions to achieve this goal. It is preferred to pray on surfaces, grounds and prayer carpets which do not disturb the person's meditation due their colors, shapes, or surface types. Another disturbance can be due to the type of material that it should not irritate the person when one touches it.

20. Abdullah bin Amr said: "I saw Rasulullah ﷺ praying both with and without wearing shoes" [1] (653).

Commentary:

It is established in different legal schools of prayer in Islam that the person should pray without any shoes. However, there are cases and instances of this rule that the person can pray without removing his or her shoes according the practice of Rasulullah ﷺ. A person can pray with or without regular socks.

21. If the person knew what type of act one is doing by passing in front of a praying person, then, this person will wait for forty. This will be better for this person than passing in front of a praying person [6] [1] [2] (261).

Commentary:

As in the above narration, it is discouraged to pass in front of a praying person. When the person is trying to focus, a person passing in front of this person distracts him or her. Therefore, it is suggested to put something in the front as a barrier[14] while praying. Rasulullah ﷺ suggests to wait if he or she wants to pass in front of a praying person. The seriousness of this in the above narration is expressed with the number forty. The narrator in the above saying of Rasulullah ﷺ adds that "I don't know if Rasulullah ﷺ said forty days, months or years." In any case, when the praying person is done with his or her prayer then this person can pass. Distracting a praying person and not respecting them during this act is a big deal as it is underlined by Rasulullah ﷺ that the person would wait for forty days, months or years if he or she knows the seriousness of it. The concept of modern day minute being 60 seconds or hour being 60 minutes were not used at that time. Therefore, the only possibility of renderings can be with days, months or years as expressed above.

---

14. sutra

22. When a person wants to pray, one should put an item in front oneself. If the person cannot find anything then one should put a stick. If the person cannot find this also, at least, he or she should draw a line in one's front before starting the prayer. After this, if any person passes in front of this praying person, it won't harm or distract this person [1](689) [10].

Commentary:

Rasulullah ﷺ in the above narration gives some practical solutions to remove the obsession of oneself trying to focus during the prayer and not to be disturbed from their surroundings. This type of attitude can make the person please Allah سبحانه وتعالى when one has the intention of following the way of Rasulullah ﷺ in Islam. At a practical level, there are a lot of people who could be considered as perfectionists with the extreme issue of obsession. Therefore, in the prayers, these practical teachings of the religion can make the worship regular, easy and applied in the daily life of a person.

23. Abu Humayd Saidi said: When Rasulullah ﷺ used to pray, he used to turn towards the direction of kiblah and raised his hands to start the prayer by saying "Allah سبحانه وتعالى is the Greatest and Exalted [5]."

24. Muhammad ibn Maslama said: when Rasulullah ﷺ stood up to pray an optional prayer, Rasulullah ﷺ used to say: "Allah سبحانه وتعالى is the Greatest and the Exalted. I turned my face as the believer of One Creator (Hanif) who created the skies and the earth. I am not from the ones who are not believers and associating partners with Allah سبحانه وتعالى [9]."

Commentary

Although there is no direction to turn while praying for Allah سبحانه وتعالى, Rasulullah turned towards a specific direction referred as Kiblah in order to establish a structured and unified practice. In the second narration above, it explains how Rasulullah practices this notion in the prayer as well. Although there is a physical specific directional posture in the prayer which is the Kiblah, one should always remember that Allah سبحانه وتعالى is beyond the limits, and directions.

---

25. One day, Rasulullah was looking at the Kabah and said: How great you are! How great your respect is! But, a believer is more respectful for Allah سبحانه وتعالى, the Exalted than you [4].

Commentary

Along with the previous narrations, one can review this narration as well. A Muslim turns toward the Kabah while praying and this direction is called Kiblah. The Kabah is one of the greatest sacred items for Muslims. The Kabah was believed to be built either by Prophet Adam or Abraham according to the scholars. Every year, millions of Muslims visit the Kabah as the fulfillment of the sacred pilgrimage. But, still Rasulullah has recognized and established a rule among his followers and humanity that a life is more important than a sacred building for Allah سبحانه وتعالى. In other words, one can review human history on the unfortunate results of bloodshed due to land, building and wealth related occupations and wars.

---

26. When the imam, the lead in the prayer says "amen", then follow him and also say "amen." When the persons saying of "amen" is agreed and coincides with the angel's confirmation of "amen" at this time, then this person's sins are forgiven [6] [2] (410).

Commentary

The above narration is related to the first chapter of the Quran that a Muslim is required to read every day in one's five time prayers. This is a seven-line chapter and is translation is:

In the name of Allah, the All Merciful, the Very Merciful

All praise and all appreciation belongs to Allah.
Allah, the Originator, the Upholder and the Maintainer of all the universes, heavens and galaxies,
Allah, the All Merciful, the Very Merciful
Allah, the only Authority and Decision Maker of the Day of Accountability.

Allah, You alone, we do worship, and
Allah, from You alone, we do seek help.

Oh Allah! guide us to the continuous permanent correct and straight path
Oh Allah! to the path of those on whom You have showered Your Grace and Blessings,
Oh Allah! not to the path of those who are disrespectful of You,
Oh Allah! not to the path of those who are on the wrong path.
Amen. [1:1-7] [13]

The name of above chapter is called Fatiha or chapter of opening. This chapter is similar to the Lord's Prayer[15] in Christianity. In the above narration, as one can see the content of this chapter from the Quran, it is a prayer and a covenant that a Muslim is expected to remind herself or himself throughout the day many times in the five times prayers. The ending of this chapter with the word and proclamation "Amen" has the same rendering as in Christianity and Judaism. The person is asking and requesting from Allah سبحانه وتعالى to accept one's prayer. The Prophet Muhammad encourages Muslims to say "amen" because there is higher possibility of the prayer being accepted by Allah سبحانه وتعالى as it is performed collectively with other humans, beings and angels.

---

15. Matthew 6:9-13

27. Abu Hurayrah narrated that Rasulullah ﷺ used to read in the optional[16] early morning prayer[17], the two short chapters from the Quran, al kafirun and al- ikhlas [2] (726).

Commentary

Below are the translations of these two chapters. It is interesting in the first chapter, al-kafirun, that it is a reminder for the person as he or she wakes up that the person will meet and encounter different people and experience instances that one may not agree with their beliefs. This chapter is reminding that one should still maintain dialogue, tolerance and acceptance although one may not agree by recognizing their positions. The second chapter, al-ikhlas, again is read early in the morning, establishes and renews one genuine faith with Allah سبحانه وتعالى that Allah سبحانه وتعالى is One and Unique. It is a reminder and refreshment of the core of the Muslim creed.

Kafirun: Dialogue, Tolerance, Acceptance
Say: Oh the ones who do not recognize and accept Allah!
I do not worship and believe yours and
You do not worship and believe mine

And You do not worship and believe mine
And I do not worship and believe yours and

Your belief and worship is yours and
My belief and worship is mine
[109: 1-6]

This chapter establishes a ground for dialogue, tolerance and acceptance for different people with different beliefs in a society. People can have differences. Although one does not have the same way of norms, having respect to each other is critical.

---

16. Two rakat sunnah prayer
17. fajr

Ikhlas: Sincerity and Unity

Say:

Allah is One.

Allah does not need anything or anyone but everything and
everyone needs Allah.

Allah does neither have any parents nor any children.

Allah is Unique, not like any human, not like any creation.

There is no equivalent to Allah

[112:1-4]

One of the key chapters in the Quran is the chapter of sincerity/unity
(Ikhlas). It is a key chapter in establishing a Union with the person and
Allah سبحانه وتعالى. Muslims rationalize, experience and vocalize this
chapter in their prayers. They especially expand the understanding
of the key expression "La ilaha illa Allah." According to the Prophet
Muhammad ﷺ, this one line chapter has a value for Allah سبحانه وتعالى
almost equivalent to one third of the full scripture of the Quran. The
reason is that this chapter presents the about of Allah سبحانه وتعالى.
Therefore, Rasulullah ﷺ recommends this chapter along with the last
two chapters of the Quran to read them three times, blow into the
hands and wipe the hands to whole body for protection and blessing.
This Quranic chapter also has two unique names of Allah سبحانه وتعالى:
Samad and Ahad. Samad is a term only used for Allah سبحانه وتعالى. It
does not have any popular usage in the language. It generally translates
as the One who does not need anything, but everyone and everything
needs Allah سبحانه وتعالى. It is also interesting to note that Samadhi as a
word is one of the last stages that is attained in Hinduism, Buddhism,
Jainismand Sikhism. In Islam, a person could be denoted as a servant of
the Samad [13].

28. Abu Zumayr narrates that one day we went outside walking with Rasulullah ﷺ. Rasulullah ﷺ saw a man praying to Allah سبحانه وتعالى insistently and persistently asking Allah سبحانه وتعالى for a solution to one of his problems. Rasulullah ﷺ said "Allah سبحانه وتعالى will certainly answer his prayer if the man ends with a stamp and a seal. "A man among us asked Rasulullah ﷺ: how can he stamp and seal it? Rasulullah ﷺ replied "By saying and ending his prayer with "Amen." [1].

Commentary

As one can understand from the above narration, there is an etiquette of praying to Allah ﷺ. The person first collects her or himself spiritually that one is in front of Allah ﷺ and asking from the All Powerful One, Allah ﷺ, who can do anything beyond the reasons and natural laws. Then, the person starts the prayer by accepting one's position in front of Allah ﷺ, appreciating Allah ﷺ with humbleness and humility and asking forgiveness for any shortcomings and evil engagements. Then, the person remembers and sends salawat to Rasulullah ﷺ and all the other messengers and appreciating their teachings. Then, the person now can ask Allah ﷺ for what he or she wants good in this world and afterlife with humbleness, humility and sincerity. After insistently asking as a method of discharge, now the person can close the prayer by again sending salawat, with an appreciation of Rasulullah ﷺ, the teacher. The last statement can be the expression "amen" as a stamp and a seal as similar to a person mailing an important package with express mail which the person expects the delivery with certainty and insurance.

29. The praying person is in the state of calling to their Hearing, Caring, Responding, and Merciful God. Therefore, the person should be careful in what state he or she is calling Allah ﷺ, and he or she should not read the scripture, the Quran loudly with the intention of showing off and arrogance, [10] (344).

Commentary

When a person prays and calls Allah ﷻ, Allah ﷻ is always there, present, active, hearing, caring, and responding to the person with mercy. Therefore, the person should focus his or her inner state that this person is in dialogue and conversation with Allah ﷻ. In this perspective, the person should always be respectful, humble and appreciative in these state of verbal, mindful and spiritual engagements while conversing with Allah ﷻ. One can also read scripture, the Quran. Reading and recitation of the Quran constantly is a very common practice among Muslims. It is common that Muslims try to finish portions of the Quran daily in their schedule as a worship either in a formal prayer or outside the formal prayer while sitting, lying down, walking even driving. However, according to the above saying of Rasulullah ﷺ, this engagement should also be with pure intention of benefiting oneself but not showing piety for others.

---

30. Qatadah asked Anas: with which supplication did Rasulullah ﷺ used to pray to Allah ﷻ most of the time? Anas said: "Oh Allah! Grant and give us good and blessings in this world and in the afterlife and protect us from the punishment of fire, [2] (2690).

Commentary

Above is one of the most famous supplications that Muslims constantly recite. This prayer is mentioned in the Quran. As Rasulullah ﷺ shows all the applications of the Quran in his practice and in his teachings, this can be one of the examples. To allude to this fact, one of the titles of Rasulullah ﷺ was "the walking Quran." Rasulullah ﷺ always teaches to ask from Allah ﷻ having an easy and good life in this world and afterlife. If a person asks difficulty in life with a good intention of pleasing Allah ﷻ, a person may not be able to handle the trials and tests given by Allah ﷻ. Therefore, one should always remember their weakness with humility and humbleness in front of Allah ﷻ and ask easiness with blessings from Allah ﷻ in this world and afterlife as instructed by Rasulullah ﷺ. The narrator Anas was a person who lived with Rasulullah ﷺ for a long time with his choice in order to learn from him. Anas is one of the famous narrators from Rasulullah ﷺ in the hadith tradition.

31. Abu Malik reported from his father that when a person became Muslim, Rasulullah ﷺ used to teach this person how to pray five times a day and also taught this person the supplication: "Oh Allah! My Sustainer! Forgive me! Shower Your Mercy and Blessings on me! Constantly guide me to the correct and true path! Protect me! Shower on me easiness, sustenance, and abundant bounties! [2] (2697R1).

Commentary

Above practice of Rasulullah ﷺ shows the importance of the five regular prayers. When a person becomes Muslim, the most important part is the five-times daily prayers that can help the person maintain a regular relationship with Allah ﷻ and keep the person on the path. In this regard, the above supplication is critical to ask constant guidance, blessings and easiness from Allah ﷻ for one's worldly life and afterlife. It is important to realize that Rasulullah ﷺ does not instruct a beginner in religion with the prohibitions of the religion but first alludes to the practice that one should first establish a regular connection with Allah ﷻ through daily prayers. The restrictions instructed by religion can follow when the person gets grounded in their relationship with Allah ﷻ.

32. One day, Abu Bakr asked Rasulullah ﷺ: "teach me a supplication that I can recite in my prayers." Rasulullah ﷺ said: "say!, Oh My Sustainer and Nourisher, I oppressed myself many times with sins, rebelling against You. No one can forgive those sins except You. Please forgive me with a forgiveness from You. Have mercy on me. Indeed, and certainly, You are the Most Forgiving, Accepter of Repentance and the Most Merciful and the Most Gracious," [2] (2705).

Commentary

The above suggested prayer is recommended for Muslims to say in their five daily prayers. One can analyze one's ideal relationship with Allah ﷻ from the above prayer suggested by Rasulullah ﷺ. A person goes through different bad and ill spiritual discourses throughout the day. These can be through verbal engagements, actions or thoughts or feelings. One can call them as sins in their technical religious word. When a person embodies this character then, this is the first step to correct oneself. Because there is the One, God, who knows the person's all internal and external, public and secret engagements. How can a person be honest with oneself if he or she claims that this person did not have those evil and sick spiritual engagements? Therefore, in Islam, supplication and prayers are the means that embody this honest disposition of the person in front of Allah ﷻ against one's continuous evil and sick spiritual renderings. It is required in Islam to keep the private and secret confession with Allah ﷻ but not with humans. In this regard, a person is expected to discharge and empty oneself through tears, self-reflection, repentance and regret. This attitude is the essence of one's elevation in front of Allah ﷻ. It is interesting to note that this remark is made to Abu Bakr considered as the highest ranking disciple of the Prophet Muhammad ﷺ. Sometimes, Rasulullah ﷺ mentioned a topic to a person who already had the embodiment of this suggested or implied trait. This can be considered as another way of praising the person for their spiritual level with Allah ﷻ. In this regard, Abu Bakr, a person constantly worried about his relationship with Allah ﷻ, did truly embody this supplication in his life. He was known to be one of the disciples who cried a lot in his prayers discharging himself in front of Allah ﷻ. He did not talk much and always preferred silence as a lifestyle next to Rasulullah ﷺ. There is a famous aphorism for him that he was the image of the Prophet Muhammad ﷺ without the prophethood from God.

33. Aisha, the wife of Rasulullah ﷺ said, Rasulullah ﷺ used to supplicate Allah ﷻ as: "Oh my God, my Sustainer and Nourisher! I take refuge in You from the trials of the fire, the punishment of the fire, the trials of life after death in purgatory, the punishment of life after death in purgatory, from the evils of wealth and poverty and I ask refuge in You from the evils of the antichrist [2] (589R1).

Commentary

It is important to ask constantly to Allah ﷻ and take refuge in Allah ﷻ from possible future evil trials and accountability according to the above testimony of Rasulullah ﷺ. In this regard, the above supplication is a very famous one practiced among Muslims. It is interesting to note that there is taking refuge from something due to potential unexpected trials. After these trials, the suffering and punishment follows. In this regard, the word "fitnah" in Arabic is translated as trials. In its etymology, it can represent any source of power that one may not anticipate or predict its after-effect. One can call this in physics, maybe, a chaotic state. In this regard in Arabic, fire is associated with the same word. A young person with the power of youth is named with this word because youth represents strength with uncontrolled emotions. An unpredicted social turmoil is named with this word as well in Arabic language.

As one can see, wealth and poverty can be an evil or a blessing for some people. It is important to ask protection from the evil outcomes of both according to the above supplication. There is a similar understanding and belief in Christ and the antichrist in Islam as in Christianity. In addition, in Islam, there are a lot of details and explanations of them through the teachings of Rasulullah ﷺ. One of the teachings for different reports of the time of antichrist is that there would be a lot of trials and evils and people often would have hard time to distinguish the truth or facts from wrong or falsehood. In this regard, Rasulullah ﷺ teaches Muslims to ask help from Allah ﷻ for the expected evil renderings of this time. Lastly, the belief in purgatory is somewhat similar and different than the belief of it compared to some denominations of Christianity. In Islam, as soon as the person dies, there is either the life of Heaven or punishment which starts immediately after the initial questioning of the angels in purgatory. So, purgatory is a temporal waiting place of the person until the Day of Judgment. Here, the concepts of time and space are different for the deceased as the person is in another dimension than from ours.

34. Before you go to bed for sleeping make wudhu, ablution as if you would pray [2] (2710).

Commentary

Daily human needs can be transformed into a form of worship if one follows the teachings of Rasulullah ﷺ. In the case of sleep, a person possibly relieving oneself and washing up as a ritual of wudhu before going to bed can be considered in worship during one's sleep due to the intention of following the teachings of Rasulullah ﷺ. If one does these practices due to the sole intention of their health practices, they can have the health benefits but this person can be deprived of the rewards of worship from Allah ﷻ. The person should do it due to the practice of Rasulullah ﷺ as a ritual. Then, health benefits follow as well with its worship fulfilments.

35. Before you go to bed for sleeping make wudhu, ablution as if you would pray. Then, lie down on the bed at your right side and recite: "Oh My God, my Sustainer and Nourisher! I turn my face towards You and submitted myself to You. I trusted You with all my affairs, activities, business, dealings and matters. I take refuge and rely on You with solace, hope, love, and respect. There is no alternative and security except You [2] (2710).

Commentary

The above narration is the continuation of the previous narration. Rasulullah ﷺ teaches the position of sleep in the bed to be on the right side of the body and right hand under the face. Then, there are the statements of supplications to express the weakness and vulnerability of a person during sleep. Before transiting into the stage of sleep, the person accepts his or her position of vulnerability and submits fully to Allah ﷻ as the Creator Who does not sleep but is Alive, Watching and Protecting. In this regard, a person discharges oneself from all worries of engagements and relies on Allah ﷻ as the Care Taker.

36. Al-Bara mentioned that whenever Rasulullah ﷺ used to go to bed for sleeping he used to say "Oh my God, my Sustainer and Nourisher! I become alive and death with Your Name." When Rasulullah ﷺ used to wake up from sleep he used to say "All thanks and gratitude is to Allah ﷻ Who made us alive after our death. Our return is to Allah ﷻ." [2] (2711).

Commentary

According to the above testimony of Rasulullah ﷺ, sleeping is similar to death. This is also mentioned in the Quran. The Quran states [14]:

> "It is Allah ﷻ [alone that has this power—Allah ﷻ] who causes all human beings to die at the time of their [bodily] death, and [causes to be as dead], during their sleep, those that have not yet died: thus, Allah ﷻ withholds [from life] those upon whom Allah ﷻ has decreed death, and lets the others go free for a term set [by Allah ﷻ). In [all] this, behold, there are messages indeed for people who think!"[18]

Therefore, a person prepares oneself for a quasi-death state with the engagement of sleeping. In this regard, every day, a new wake-up is a rehearsal of becoming alive from death. The final death and becoming alive in front of Allah ﷻ is stated with the expression "Our return is to Allah ﷻ." One can also realize that the relationship with the Quranic verse and the statement of Rasulullah ﷺ in the above case. Rasulullah ﷺ practically shows how the Quranic teachings can be applied in a Muslim's life. Therefore, both the Quran and the hadith have a complimentary role of learning and practicing Islam in a Muslim's life.

---

18. [39:42]

37. Oh my God, Sustainer and Nourisher of the skies, galaxies and systems, Sustainer and Nourisher of the earth, Sustainer and Nourisher of the Great Dominion and Authority, oh our Sustainer and Nourisher, Oh Sustainer and Nourisher of everything, the One Who gives the force to split a seed and grow it, the One who cleaves the grain and the fruit-kernel asunder the One Who sent Bible: the Gospel, the Psalms, and the Torah, and the Quran, I seek refuge in You from the evil of everything that You hold from their necks, that You control [2] (2713).

Commentary

The above prayer is recommended by Rasulullah 🪽 to perform in the bed before one falls asleep. As one can realize the highly penetrating and strong wordings about Allah 🪽 that one can somewhat comprehend the interaction and relationship between the Infinite Powerful Merciful Creator and weak and incapable humans. The etiquette of praying to Allah 🪽 in Islam first requires one to declare from whom the person is asking their needs. All the above statements are truth and facts about Allah 🪽 through the approaches of the human language and discourses. One should remember that there is always reductionism by humans at the interface of the divine transcendent realities.

Another interesting point is that the reminder of the attribution of Allah 🪽 as the Sender of the Bible: the Gospel, the Psalms, and the Torah before the person sleeps according to the above testimony of Rasulullah 🪽. One may expect that before a Muslim sleeps the identity relationship of the follower of the person with Islam and the Quran would be more emphasized. Yet, the inclusivity and unchanging message of Allah 🪽 is reminded from the first creation, Adam, until the End of Days. This may be reminded to the person that Allah 🪽, the Creator is the same and did not leave humans without guidance in chaos. Allah 🪽 sent constantly books such as the Bible: the Gospel, the Psalms, and the Torah, and the Quran and the messengers such as Moses (Musa) & Jesus (Isa) عليهم السلام and Muhammad 🪽. As mentioned in the previous parts, some people can view sleeping as a state of chaos similar to death due to its unknowns. In this regard, knowing the structure, the guidelines that Allah 🪽 did not leave the person by himself or herself since the time of their creation in chaos without any guidance can be very easing and comforting as a reminder. Perhaps, it is one's personal mind renderings that form and push the person in chaos, fear and insecurity when the person ignores these teachings.

---

38. Hanzala reports the following: One day I met Abu Bakr, a very close friend of Rasulullah ﷺ. Abu Bakr said: "how are you Hanzala?" then, I said: Hanzala became a hypocrite. Then, Abu Bakr said: "SubhanAllah!, All Perfection and Glory belongs to Allah!, why do you say that?" Then, I said "when we are with Rasulullah ﷺ, he tells us about the afterlife, about the Heaven, punishment and accountability. I feel that as if I see all that in front of my eyes. Then, when I leave from the presence of Rasulullah ﷺ, I have engagement with my family, kids and business. I forget most of those teachings." Then, Abu Bakr said: "Certainly and for sure, it exactly happens to me as well." Then, Abu Bakr and I went to see Rasulullah ﷺ. I said:" I became a hypocrite, Oh Messenger of Allah!" Then, Rasulullah ﷺ said: "what happened?" I said: "Oh Messenger of Allah! When we stay with you and you tell us about the accountability, penalties, rewards and Heaven in the afterlife I feel them as if I see them with my eyes. Then, when we leave from your presence, then our family, children and our work engagements preoccupy us, we forget most of those. Then, Rasulullah ﷺ said: Indeed, I swear on Allah ﷻ to whom my life and existence depends fully on, if you keep and preserve the same states of your heart and mind while you were with me and also you are in the state of constant remembrance of Allah ﷻ, then angels would shake hands with you in your beds and in all your paths. However, oh Hanzala! Take it easy, slowly, there is a time, there is a time. Rasulullah ﷺ repeated the last expression three times [2] (2750).

Commentary

The above testimony of Rasulullah ﷺ highlights multiple points. First, it is reality that the state of human heart and mind can change depending on engagements with prayers and with the company of the pious. According to some interpretations, the expression "there is a time, there is a time" can mean that there is a time for worldly affairs and there is a time for prayers and worship. It can also mean the level that one wants to reach in one's relationship with Allah ﷻ takes time and effort that the person should take it easy but in regular and continuous slow steps. Second, the above testimony shows the importance of being in good friends who would remind the person Allah ﷻ and the engagements of afterlife. This has an effect. Oppositely, there is an effect of a bad company. Third, both Hanzala and Abu Bakr were constantly monitoring their hearts' and minds' engagements and changes. This shows the importance of self-reflection in spiritual affairs in Islam.

Afterlife

Abu Zarr asked to Rasulullah ﷺ: "Oh Prophet of Allah! How about the person who loves a group of people but she or he cannot do what they do." Rasulullah ﷺ said: "Oh Abu Zarr! you will be with the people whom you love in the afterlife [1] [4].

Oppression is a darkness on the Day of Resurrection [2] (2579).

1. Abu Zarr asked to Rasulullah ﷺ: "Oh Prophet of Allah!, How about the person who loves a group of people but she or he cannot do what they do." Rasulullah ﷺ said: "Oh Abu Zarr! you will be with the people whom you love [1] [4].

Commentary

The above is a famous narration among Muslims. Abu Zarr is a person who is known to have an ascetic life. In practice, it is important to do good and ethical and at the same time, believe and appreciate Allah ﷻ sincerely and truly. Therefore, if a person for whatever reason cannot do this, having affection and love for those is the least requirement to be with this group of people in the afterlife. One of the ways to show this affinity and love is praying for these people. Another way is to praise these people even though people may think that they are bad.

2. I will be waiting for you at the special pool of kauthar [2] (2289).

Commentary

In Islam, death is not something scary but the happy time of meeting with Allah ﷻ, the Prophets and the friends of Allah ﷻ. A person will spend the most pleasurable times after death. One of these occasions will be with the Prophet Muhammad ﷺ. Rasulullah ﷺ will wait in the afterlife at a special pool named as the kauthar for the grand celebration and party. This party will be for the ones in this life:

▶ who won the struggle against their own selves and egos against their spiritual diseases
▶ who were humble
▶ who recognized only one and unique God and appreciated all the favors from Allah ﷻ by praying
▶ who were ethical, just and fair but not oppressive.

In this party, Rasulullah ﷺ describes that they will be drinking, celebrating this achievement and celebrating the retirement from all the worldly stresses, worries, insecurities, and fears. This new life will be spent in constant bodily and spiritual pleasures without death.

3. I will be waiting for you at the pool of Kawsar. While some people are coming to join the party they would be detained and stopped. Rasulullah ﷺ will say and beg: "Oh Allah! they are my friends, they are my friends" and it would be said: "You don't know what type of evil they did after you died [2] (2297)."

Commentary

This is narration is another or extended version of the previous narration. As some of the followers of Rasulullah ﷺ are planning to join the party, they will be prevented from joining it. There are different possible explanations for this narration. These people are the ones who did evil in the world and did not ask forgiveness and repentance from Allah ﷻ and from the people that they oppressed before they died.

This narration with others shows the mercy of Rasulullah ﷺ for his followers. Rasulullah ﷺ wants to do as much as possible even for the ones who were engaged in evil after the death of Rasulullah ﷺ. In some other narrations, Rasulullah ﷺ humbly begs in the position of prostration to Allah ﷻ for these people until Allah ﷻ forgives them and removes their deserved punishment due to their evil encounters on the earth. In the discipline of the science of hadith, this hadith can be an example of how one narration or statement of Rasulullah ﷺ can transmit with more or less words, sentences and details with different chains of narrators. One can review the hadith numbers two and three in this section to realize this perspective in this methodology.

4. Oppression is a darkness on the Day of Resurrection [2] (2579).

Commentary

According to the above testimony of Rasulullah ﷺ, the oppression and evil renderings of a person in this world will be darkness in the afterlife. The darkness can symbolize the accountability and punishment of the person due to one's evil or oppression. One of the greatest oppressions is the person's unrecognition, ungrateful, and unappreciative attitude toward Allah ﷻ although Allah ﷻ created the person and gave that person livelihood. In this perspective, a believer and appreciative of Allah ﷻ will have a light in the Day of Resurrection.

5. The right of each individual will be paid fully in the Day of Judgment. Even, a sheep without horn will receive its right from the one with horn [2] (2582).

Commentary

One can understand that there is an accountability after death. The accountability will be in all life engagements with details. There are some interpretations of the above narration that the animals that were oppressed in life will take their rights from others. An example as mentioned in the above testimony that a sheep with horn could have oppressed another sheep without horn in their fight or any type of engagement. Overall, the personal relevance of above narration is to encourage the person to live an ethical, just and God conscious life because there will be accountability.

6. Do you know who is the one in bankruptcy? The companions around Rasulullah ﷺ replied: "The one in bankruptcy among us is the one who does neither have a penny nor anything of worth." Then, Rasulullah ﷺ said: "Indeed, the one in bankruptcy among my people is the person who comes in the Day of Judgment with a lot of prayers, fasting, charity but this person abused others, slandered others, stole the wealth of others, shed blood, injured and killed others. In the Day of Judgment, all the good deeds of this person will be given to the ones who he or she imposed all those evil acts. At the end, if this person's good deeds finish to compensate the past evils, then the sins of others will be taken and given to this person. Then, this person will be thrown to hell for punishment" [2] (2581).

Commentary

In the above testimony of Rasulullah ﷺ, one can see the importance of ethical and moral life in Islam. The piety alone is not sufficient to please Allah ﷻ and to be in Heaven in afterlife. The true piety should accompany with ethical and moral life due to God consciousness. In other words, one of the main goals of religion in Islam is to establish just, moral and ethical life with appreciation and recognition of God. Both are required and necessary for salvation of the person in the afterlife.

7. When a man was walking on a path he saw tree branches that could possibly obstruct the pathway. He said to himself: "Indeed, I should remove those so that they don't harm people." Then, due to this action, he was accepted to Heaven [2] (1914R2).

Commentary

One can understand from above testimony of Rasulullah ﷺ that there are numerous ways to enter Heaven in Islam. For example, a person who does a service to benefit others can be granted forgiveness and pardon by Allah ﷻ and enter Heaven after death. This good deed can be as small as removing a harmful object from the path of people as mentioned in the above testimony of Rasulullah ﷺ. In this sense, after life or death is not something scary in Islam but a person who was conscious of God with appreciation and good behavior to others can enjoy a better life after death in Heaven.

8. A man swore and said: "I took an oath that indeed, Allah ﷻ is not going to forgive this person." Allah ﷻ, the Exalted said: "Who is the one who takes an oath on Me that I am not going to forgive this person. I, indeed, forgave this person and I granted pardon for his actions" [2] (2621).

Commentary

According to the above testimony of Rasulullah ﷺ, no one can take an oath about fate of the person in the afterlife. Only, Allah ﷻ knows and can judge the person. A person taking an oath about future, or about fate of a person can be in a futile position due to assuming the responsibility of Divine Authority. Assuming this position on oneself can be a full trait of conceit and arrogance. This person can be reprimanded by Allah ﷻ if the person does not ask forgiveness.

9. There is nothing heavier than a good, moral and ethical character in the Divine Accountability (4799) [1].

Commentary

In the above testimony of Rasulullah ﷺ, one of the final products of piety and relationship with Allah ﷻ in Islam is to cultivate good, ethical and moral character. In this sense, a believer cannot transfuse into the notions of piety unless one applies the good, moral and ethical behavior in one's life. There are a lot of statement about Rasulullah ﷺ related to his good, gentle, humble, and kind treatment of others. Oppositely, there are a lot of warnings of Rasulullah ﷺ about the bad, harsh, arrogant, and rude treatment of others.

10. A person with rude language, conceit and arrogance will not enter Heaven (4801) [1].

Commentary

Rasulullah ﷺ alludes to some of the signs of arrogance in one's daily conversations. One sign can be the attitude of rudeness, harshness, crudeness, or vulgarity in the way a person talks. Improper or rude toning in one's speech, or face expressions can be some other examples. Rasulullah ﷺ in this case encourages the person to stop these habits and reminds them the Divine reward system in afterlife.

11. One day, a man came to Rasulullah 🕊 and asked: "when is the
    End of Days?" Rasulullah 🕊 said: what did you prepare for it? The
    man said: "The love of Allah 🕊 and the love of Rasulullah 🕊."
    Then, Rasulullah 🕊 replied: "You will be with whom you love. [2]
    (2639)."

Commentary

This testimony of Rasulullah 🕊 is very famous among the Muslims. The
person will be with the ones who he or she loves in the afterlife. In Islam,
a true believer loves Allah 🕊 and Rasulullah 🕊 more than him or herself.
In other words, the person places the guidelines given by Allah 🕊 in the
Quran and in the teachings of the Prophet Muhammad 🕊 as a priority
in one's life. In the above narration, the man himself can be a pious or a
devout Muslim. Yet, the narration emphasizes the notion of importance
of one's inclinations in their heart towards the Divine teachings.

On another note, Rasulullah 🕊 focuses this person to the purpose and
goal rather than the means. In other words, Rasulullah 🕊 did not answer
the man's question about time of the End of Days but he asked him what
he prepared for it. In other words, there are things in life that are not at
our control. We are responsible of things that we have control over with
our free will. A person wasting his or her time with daily discourses of
current events with the news or people's affairs but not really focusing
the present time to prepare for the departure with death is considered
to be in distraction, lost, and heedlessness in Islam. Even, a person can
be distracted with religious matters if it does not serve a purpose as
mentioned in the above case.

12. One day, a man came to the mosque. He said to Rasulullah ﷺ: "Oh Messenger of Allah! When is the End of Days?" Rasulullah ﷺ replied: "What did you prepare for it?" The man said: "Oh Messenger of Allah! I did not prepare much neither from the prayers, fasting nor giving charity but I, however, love Allah ﷻ and the Messenger of Allah ﷺ." Rasulullah ﷺ then said: You will be with the ones whom you love [2] (2639R5)."

Commentary

Above is the same narration from Rasulullah ﷺ with different chain of narrators and with an addition compared to the previous one. In this narration, one can see the emphasis that the true inclination of one's heart and mind would determine final destination in the afterlife. The man perhaps mentions that he just fulfilled the minimum requirements in the religion but did not go beyond with extra prayers, much fasting or regularly helping the poor or needy. However, he mentioned that although he did not do much, but he loved Allah ﷻ and the messenger of God. In other words, he either wanted to put much effort into religious affairs but he couldn't, or, he did not want to expend much effort on religious matters but he always carried love in the form of appreciation, gratitude and thankfulness toward Allah ﷻ and the messenger of Allah ﷺ.

Knowledge

The scholars are the inheritors of the prophets [1].

1. Whoever selects and goes on a path in search of knowledge and learning, Allah ﷻ will make that path easy for this person leading him or her to Heaven [2] (2699).

Commentary:

According to the above testimony of the Prophet Muhammad ﷺ (Rasulullah ﷺ), knowledge and learning is very critical to lead a person to please Allah ﷻ and enter Heaven. It is very interesting to see the transformation of a desert society with no formal and structured education into communities developing and advancing in different natural, legal and social sciences after the introduction of Islam. One can historically view the position of scholars and their value in Muslim societies due to the strong emphasis on learning and knowledge with the teachings of the Quran and Rasulullah ﷺ.

2. The scholars are the inheritors of the prophets [1].

Commentary

The Prophet Muhammad is the last messenger of Allah ﷻ. There will not be any other messengers sent by Allah ﷻ until the end of days. Therefore, the genuine, sincere and knowledgeable scholars will act to guide and remind people about the original teachings of Rasulullah ﷺ according to the above testimony of Rasulullah ﷺ. With these qualifications of genuine, humble and compassionate practice, the scholars are expected to contextualize these sacred teachings according to the changing needs of the time and place. In this contextualizing, expertise of the discipline, and following the methodology of the canonized teachings of the creed and pillars, are guidelines in new renderings or new interpretations. Therefore, today and in the past, there have been a lot of discussions in Islamic scholarship about the acceptable or rejected innovations in practice.

3. Child Education

When your child is at the age of seven, start teaching him or her how to pray. When they become ten, then be firm with them, increase your advice and reward system and by the age of ten, and provide them with separate beds. [1]

Commentary:

Rasulullah ﷺ advises the age of seven to start children accustomed to the rituals of prayer. Depending on the child and circumstances, informal and formal learning can happen earlier as long as the children like to pray on their own initiatives. As they get close to the age of puberty, the teachings should increase with good quality education, a reward system, care and firmness. As soon as the child reaches the age of puberty, the parents become more like friends instead of authority figures. Rasulullah ﷺ also instructs the separation of beds at the age of ten as a cutoff time due to the bodily awareness of children reaching to their peak levels.

4. Allah ﷻ equipped me with guidance and knowledge and sent me to people as a source of guidance and knowledge. Learning from them is similar to the rain falling on the ground. With this rainfall: There is a good piece of land, retains the water, sucks the water itself and grows many fruits and vegetables.

Then, there is another type of concrete ground. The water does not penetrate inside but it holds and collects water similar to ponds. People benefit from this piece of land. They drink from it, they use it for watering and feeding their animals.

Then, there is another type of land. It neither grows any fruits or vegetables nor it holds water for others to benefit.

Similarly, the first one is a person who understands truly the religion of Allah ﷻ and benefits himself or herself.

The second one is the one who learns and teaches others.

The third one is the person who does not care about improving oneself, learning, and knowledge. This person does not accept the guidance of Allah ﷻ for which I was sent [2] (2282).

Commentary

Islam acknowledges that human civilizations have progressed immensely with the prophets and messengers of Allah ﷻ sent in different times in human history [15] [7]. The divine guidance through prophets and scriptures helped humans live together in civilized manners. Some of the scholars [7] argue that the emergence of humanities and liberal arts approaches of the colleges were much embedded in the teachings of all the prophets, scriptures, in the teachings of the Prophet Muhammad ﷺ and in the Quran. In the above narration, Rasulullah ﷺ encourages one to learn and benefit oneself primarily. At the second level, even though there may not be a benefit of the knowledge for oneself, it is still good to learn and teach others. This is an interesting emerging pedagogy today: the first one is holistic approach of learning, benefiting and teaching. The second one is a non-holistic approach of teaching similar to academic life in colleges and secular schools. Both efforts are encouraged by Rasulullah ﷺ. The last category is the one who does not care about learning or teaching and devalues the education of self and social improvement.

5. Anas was a teenager. His mother wanted Anas to learn from Rasulullah ﷺ. Therefore, she wanted her son to stay with Rasulullah ﷺ and shadow him while being in service to Rasulullah ﷺ. Anas reported that, "I was with Rasulullah ﷺ for nine years learning and helping him as his assistant. During this nine years, I don't remember anytime that he questioned me: "Why did you do this? Or, why didn't you do this like that?" Rasulullah ﷺ never found fault in me and never criticized me" [2] (2309).

Commentary

The above narration is from a very famous person, Anas. The above narration is also a very famous narration among Muslims that the Muslims try to take Rasulullah ﷺ as the role model in child education and human relations for the application of kindness. Anas was a teenager when he started living and observing Rasulullah ﷺ's life very closely. Therefore, there are a lot of narrations from Anas about the life of Rasulullah ﷺ. Rasulullah ﷺ was very gentle and nice in his character. His method of teaching was not in formal verbal instruction but always he was the role model for people to observe and learn. In children's education, in student teacher relationships or subordinate relationships, the above narrations teach not to be harsh and critical to any person especially to the ones with whom the person regularly interacts at work, school or home. In other narrations, people around Rasulullah ﷺ tended not to want to leave Rasulullah ﷺ, his company and presence. This was due to his charming character of calmness, gentleness, and always comforting attitude in all different conditions of conflicts in addition to his ethical and moral character of generosity, courage, and open heartedness.

6. Whatever I ask you to restrain yourself, then restrain yourself, whatever I ask you to follow and do, then do it as much as and as best as you can. The previous nations of the other prophets were harmed due to making it difficult on themselves by asking questions and were misguided from the original teachings of their prophets [2] (1337).

Commentary

Rasulullah ﷺ always encouraged for learning. One of the ways of learning is to learn by asking questions. The questions should be well intended to learn, to practice, and not to expose the faults of others. There are a lot of times that Rasulullah ﷺ answered people's questions genuinely for them to learn. One of the ways that is very important in learning is thinking, questioning and practicing knowledge. There were also other times people asked questions only to challenge but not to learn. In this case, Rasulullah ﷺ advises to follow and try to learn and implement to the best of one's ability. There were previous nations with other prophets who did not respect their messenger and humiliated them with their challenging attitudes of questioning. Therefore, Rasulullah ﷺ gives advice about this genuine methodology of learning to any person who is trying to learn as a student. In practice, it is important to wait for the answer of a question until there is a good time and place for it. A wrong question at a wrong time and a place can make the person deduce wrong meanings. These attitudes can alienate the person from genuine learning. Another genuine way of learning is to spend a good amount of time with the teacher and to learn and to observe natural discourses, occurring events and deduce meanings from them. Therefore, most of the people spent a lot of time with Rasulullah ﷺ in order to learn everything in its context with its application. Today, one may call this methodology of learning as ethnography or participant observation: applied and relevant learning. Most of the companions of Rasulullah ﷺ learned with this methodology. Rasulullah ﷺ most of the time did not lecture with question and answers as the considered traditional way of teaching in our times. He acted as a role model with the divine teachings and lived the teachings in his own life. People observed him and practiced accordingly. There were times that he did explain in detail and answered the questions as well. In the Prophetic teachings and practice, any unused knowledge can be considered as distraction, waste of time and waste of one's effort. In other words, a person learns in order to benefit themselves and practice with this knowledge. Therefore, there is the prayer of Rasulullah ﷺ "Oh Allah! I ask refuge in You from the knowledge that is not beneficial" [9].

Purification of the Heart

For sure, Allah does not value your bodily appearances or
externalities but Allah gives value what is in your heart
and accordingly, values your actions. Real love and fear
(taqwa) is here, pointing his chest towards his heart. [1]
[5] [6] [2] (2564).

1. Intention

    The reward of all the actions will be given according to the person's
    intentions [6] [2] .

Commentary

In Islam, the intention of the person is very the essence of all the actions.
The result of one's engagement is given according to their intention.
Praying to Allah ﷻ, helping others, charity and honesty are all judged
according to one's intentions.

2. Heart

    For sure, Allah does not value your bodily appearances or
    externalities but Allah values what is in your heart and accordingly,
    values your actions. Real love and fear (taqwa) is here! (pointing
    his chest towards his heart.) [6] [2] [1] [4] (2564).

Commentary

The purpose of religion is to remove all the spiritual defects in one's
heart. Through the Divine commands, Islam prescribes prayers, fasting,
charity and other teachings to instill and to inculcate the true meanings

of sincerity, sacrifice, and honesty. The happiness in this world and after life comes with the true implementation of these teachings. The essence of worship and religious guidelines, some people may call it as shariah, in Islam is built one's upright ethical and moral character. In the above testimony, Rasulullah ﷺ underlines this essence of the religion. In Islam, the virtue, ethical behavior and character are all struggle that constantly comes in different human dealings. These dealings can be worship, prayer, business transactions, learning, marriage, social engagement or kinship relations. It is required to perform good actions in Islam. The intention of all these dealings is expected to be pure. The intention should not be interest based, love of someone or something, or fears or expectations but it should be due to one's relationship with Allah ﷻ, to please, to appreciate and to thank Allah ﷻ for all favors.

3. Anger: Rasulullah ﷺ asked: "Who is the strongest? "The companions replied as:" the one who is most strong physically." Rasulullah ﷺ said: "The strongest is the one who can control his or her anger" [2] (2558).

Commentary

One of the teachings that Rasulullah ﷺ brought to implement as a change in the pre-Islamic society was the management of anger. Rasulullah ﷺ did not get angry for unnecessary and futile incidents. When there were incidents related to injustice, the signs of anger could be understood from his face but he still managed his anger and acted with logic and wisdom to remove the evil. In other narrations, Rasulullah ﷺ gave some practical and simple solutions to manage one's anger. These solutions include washing oneself spiritually[19], changing one's position such as, if one is standing then to sit, if one is sitting then to lie down. Another suggestion is to leave the scene of the anger.

---

19. Wudhu

4. Do not carry and domesticate anger and hatred, do not keep jealousy, do not keep enmity but be brothers and sisters as the servants and creation of Allah ﷻ. It is not lawful for a Muslim, a believer of Allah ﷻ, to cut relations with a brother or sister more than three days [2] (2559).

Commentary

In the above testimony of Rasulullah ﷺ, Rasulullah ﷺ instructs people to remove the spiritual diseases in one's heart from anger, hatred, jealousy, and enmity. In case the person falls short and is upset with another fellow, Rasulullah ﷺ prohibits as a religious teaching not to extend this type of estrangement from another person more than three days. Therefore, it is a common practice among Muslims to remind each other of this rule as a way of advice if someone is severing relations with another person.

5. The doors are opened in two days of the week, Monday and Thursday. Allah ﷻ forgives everyone who truly believes in One Creator. Except the two persons who have some type of ill-feelings toward each other. Then, it will be said to them: Look at each other until you remove your ill-feelings from your heart! Look at each other until you remove your ill-feelings from your heart! Look at each other until you remove your ill-feelings from your heart! [2] (2565).

Commentary

The above testimony of Rasulullah ﷺ is about a future incident that is going to happen after death. This case shows the seriousness of the effort of not having any type of ill-feelings towards one another. In other words, it is expected to remove all types negative feelings such as hatred, hostility, and ill feeling towards others before one dies. Rasulullah ﷺ repeated his statement three times in the above report. This was one of the teaching methods of Rasulullah ﷺ. When there was an important teaching of the religion, Rasulullah ﷺ used to repeat it so that the listeners could embody this teaching.

6. The strong man is not the one who wins in a fight. The strong man is the person who controls his or her anger [2] (2609).

Commentary

In Islam, all the traits of humans are given for a purpose by Allah ﷻ. All the intrinsic qualities have a purpose and a correct place and a time for its use. For the case of anger, one is supposed to show anger against injustice as a motivating force to establish peace, justice, structure and order. A person can get angry in other venues but he or she should have the skills to control it. If not, the anger of a person can lead to oppression, injustice, and evil. In a pre-Islamic society, the tribal and patriarchal norms were on the pillars of heroism and physical strength. In the above testimony of Rasulullah ﷺ, Rasulullah ﷺ re-defines the "strong man" as the one who can control anger.

7. "Oh Allah! I ask a covenant from you please do not turn me down. That is:

> I am a human being. Whoever from the believers, I caused hardships, or I got angry at them, or I said something bad at them, or I touched or hit them, please make for them this, as a source of blessing, purification, and nearness to You on the Day of Judgment [2] (2601R2).

Commentary

With all the testimonies of Rasulullah ﷺ about establishing virtue through ethics and morality, if someone makes a mistake as the normal trait of being a human, then it is important to recognize and pray to Allah ﷻ for the well-being of this person. In other words, Rasulullah ﷺ sets a role model in the application of humanly endeavors. With all the mechanisms of self-control in the teachings of Islam and the positive effect of regular prayers, there may be still occasions that the person can still do something evil. At this point, it is important take an immediate stance of recognition of this, asking forgiveness from the person and

Allah 🙠 for this engagement. Moreover, a person in Islamic tradition can try to payback or recompense another person by praying to Allah 🙠 for the well-being of this person in this world and afterlife.

---

8. Rasulullah 🙠 narrated that when Allah 🙠 created and shaped Adam in Heaven Allah 🙠 left him there. Then, Satan came wandering around Adam. Satan was trying to understand Adam's composition. When Satan realized that there is a hollow in him, Satan understood that human is a type of creation who does not have much control on him or herself [2] (2611).

Commentary

The above is an interesting narration about the essence of humans. In other words, it states that humans have powers, passions, or instincts which can be very strong. If the person does not put them under control, then the person can be puffed up with vain desires and passions as mentioned with the word hollow. Some scholars interpret the word as hollow literally with the meaning of the stomach of the person. In that case, one's lack of control over eating habits can destroy the person spiritually and physically.

---

9. When the person says "people are destroyed then", the person himself is destroyed in reality [2] (2623).

Commentary

The above testimony from Rasulullah 🙠 shows the attitude of not blaming others, thinking good about them and always praying for their well and ethical dispositions. In other words, when a person includes everyone as being destroyed but seeing oneself or their group to be saved, then this attitude itself is a destructive position in one's relationship with Allah 🙠, because, the essence of religion is well wishing for others, praying for a positive change but not asking damnation or destruction for them.

10. When one of you becomes angry and if the person is standing, then one should sit. If one still is seating and becomes angry, then he or she should lie down [2] (4782).

Commentary

The previous narrations from Rasulullah ﷺ mentioned some conceptual understanding about anger as one of the diseases of the heart. The above narration alludes to some practical advises to manage anger. In the above narration, one can see that there is an instruction to passivize oneself when one is angry and not continue in the engagement.

11. Anger is from Satan. Satan is from fire. The fire is extinguished by water. When one of you becomes angry he or she should make ablution with water [1] (4784).

Commentary

The above testimony of Rasulullah ﷺ about anger is very interesting. It again shows a practical way of helping someone in the state of anger. When a person makes ablution[20] then this person takes another practical step to stop one's dominant urge to act on negative emotions. In all discourses, the person really believes wholeheartedly in all the teachings of the Quran and Rasulullah ﷺ to see their effects according to the scholars.

12. Whoever is deprived of gentleness and kindness then this person is deprived of all the good [1] (4809).

Commentary

After the narrations about gentleness, Rasulullah ﷺ underlines the importance in essence of the ideal communication and deliverance. The

20. wudhu

method of communicating with people can be more important than its content. In other words, the person should be gentle and kind then all the good can follow. The Quran suggests that the person should be gentle while helping others who are in need [2:263]. If the one helps others, it is better for this person to smile and make the other person comfortable rather than giving them money in a harsh manner.

---

13. There is at times some sort of shade in my heart, and I seek forgiveness from Allah سبحانه وتعالى a hundred times a day [2] (2702).

Commentary

Rasulullah ﷺ had a continuous communion and union with Allah سبحانه وتعالى. If there is a second or a feeling of blurring of this blessed communion, Rasulullah ﷺ mentions that he asks from Allah سبحانه وتعالى forgiveness at least hundred times a day. Although Rasulullah ﷺ had a very intimate and unceasing relationship with Allah سبحانه وتعالى even during his sleep, and protected and guided consistently by Allah سبحانه وتعالى, he also asked forgiveness from Allah سبحانه وتعالى as a human for possible undesired renderings. In this perspective, the followers of Rasulullah ﷺ take their time especially during and after the regular daily prayers, before and after sunset to ask forgiveness from Allah سبحانه وتعالى as practiced and embodied by Rasulullah ﷺ. In another perspective, Rasulullah ﷺ also teaches the importance of awareness of one's heart if there is anything undesired in it, the person should remove these feelings, thoughts and renderings by asking forgiveness as a means of cleansing of one's heart. It is well known that asking forgiveness[21] from Allah سبحانه وتعالى cleans the heart. One of the famous chants practiced by Muslims is the phrase of astagfirullah which means "Oh Allah! please forgive me with my all renderings and engagements with my eyes, ears, organs, mind, heart, thoughts and feelings." It is common to chant this phrase after each regular prayers and 100 times daily.

---

21. istigfar in Ar.

Ethics & Morality

The best of you is the one who is the best in character [2] (2321).

1. A believer in Allah سبحانه وتعالى is the one whom others are safe from his or her physical and verbal harm, oppression, transgression, slandering and backbiting [6] [2] (40).

Commentary

A believer is a person who does not say or do evil to hurt others. A true believer believes in Allah سبحانه وتعالى and is ashamed of oppressing others. This person knows that Allah سبحانه وتعالى is aware of everyone's actions and can do anything at any time to recompense them. People are comfortable with this person's presence. They have trust in him or her. One of the titles of Rasulullah ﷺ before the prophethood was "the one trusted." Rasulullah ﷺ used to solve conflicts among people.

2. The best of you is the one who is the best in character [2] (2321).

Commentary

One of the goals of Rasulullah ﷺ was to bring ethics and morality through the teachings of the revelation. Rasulullah ﷺ invited people for pure monotheism, justice, equal rights and the belief in accountability in the afterlife. Therefore, one can find a lot of sayings of Rasulullah ﷺ in which he praises different individuals for their upright moral and ethical characters. Rasulullah ﷺ publicizes these individuals with their names to encourage others for them to adopt these qualities as well.

3. If the parties are truthful in a business transaction, then there will be proliferation and blessing in it. If either party lies and hides anything the blessing will be blocked out [2]. (1532)

Commentary

There are various verses in the Quran and in the sayings of the Prophet Muhammad ﷺ to embody ethics in all different parts of life. The chapter 83 of the Quran is dedicated to the teachings of prevention of cheating in business transactions. Oppositely, there are numerous sayings of Rasulullah ﷺ for a fair and just businessman who will be rewarded similar to the pious people due to their sound ethics. Therefore, the above saying alludes to this notion that although the person may think he or she can gain more by cheating but in reality this person loses.

4. Whoever eats these two vegetables (pointing to garlic and onion) should not attend with its smell to our mosques and masjids. If you need to eat it and go to the mosque to pray, then one should minimize their smell by eating it in their cooked forms not raw forms [1] (1389) & [10] (IV,19).

Commentary

Rasulullah ﷺ is very particular about establishing group and social gatherings with respect and without any disturbance to each other. Even at a level of bad smell, if one has eaten a food with an unpleasant smell such as garlic or onion, then it is better for that person to pray at home instead of praying in the mosque, in a group. From this narration, the Islamic legal scholars have deduced that the people who may have bad smells due to the type of their occupation, then they also should preferably pray at their homes instead of attending the mosques with their work clothes. Rasulullah ﷺ did not prefer to eat onion and garlic due to his regular meetings with the angels. He did not want to disturb them with bad smell as angels are known to like good scents in Islamic tradition. Rasulullah ﷺ did not prohibit Muslims eating garlic or onion.

5. Taking shower on Fridays, cleaning the teeth and mouth with the toothbrush such as miswak and applying some nice perfume and scent on the body and clothes are essential.

Commentary

Rasulullah ﷺ requires all the Muslims to take shower at least once a week before going to group prayer on Fridays in the mosques. It is a revolutionary idea to systematize the life of very early Muslims who were Arabs living in the desert life conditions. One can see that Rasulullah ﷺ instructs and teaches the Muslims the daily personal and social needs of a person besides the requirements of the belief and practices of the religion. If a person does these natural human needs with the intention of following the instructions of Rasulullah ﷺ, Allah سبحانه وتعالى also rewards them as if they are worshipping Allah سبحانه وتعالى. In other words, in Islam, the intention is the key. A person can transform daily human needs of eating, cleaning, socializing, and even having an intimate relationship with the spouse into a worship in Allah سبحانه وتعالى with their intention. This intention can be to fulfill one's humanly needs in clean, ethical and moral manners through following the teachings of Rasulullah ﷺ so that one can advance and perfect one's relationship with Allah سبحانه وتعالى.

6. There was a person who saw Rasulullah ﷺ kissing his grandson, Hasan. Then, this person said: "I have ten children. I never kissed any of them." Then, Rasulullah ﷺ said: "the person who does not show mercy, then no mercy is shown to that person" [2] (2318).

Commentary

In the pre-Islamic society of patriarchy and androcentric values, one of the misinterpreted notion was courage, bravery and nobility. The misinterpretation of the "real man" in that society was not to show any mercy, caring or love to their children. Being tough and harsh towards the children were considered a noble quality of the man. When

Rasulullah ﷺ shattered these values in his own personal practice as a role model and teacher with the teachings of Islam there were many shocking moments for the people. Rasulullah ﷺ brought especially revolutionary values about children, women and slavery.

---

7. Anas reports that there was a lady who had some problem, came, and said to Rasulullah ﷺ: "Oh Prophet of Allah! I have a problem that I want to talk to you about." Rasulullah ﷺ replied to her by referring to her with the name of her child: "Which side of the road you want me to wait for you so that you can talk to me about your problem." Then, Rasulullah ﷺ went on one side of the road and the lady talked to Rasulullah ﷺ privately and helped with her problem [2] (2326).

Commentary

One can realize that Rasulullah ﷺ had an informal open door policy for everyone while Rasulullah ﷺ was still the president and in full authority of a powerful country. At that time, the new Muslim authority was ruling a few countries of our time. Rasulullah ﷺ did not have any security and bodyguards constantly walking with him. The people desired to be around him to benefit from the opportunity of being with Rasulullah ﷺ due to the immeasurable blessing, learning and practice. In the above case, the lady had a problem and wanted to talk with Rasulullah ﷺ privately and but not in public. Rasulullah ﷺ realized this and helped with her problem by talking to her on the side of the road where people could not hear. By replying to her with the name of her child, which is common in Arabic language, Rasulullah ﷺ perhaps tried to comfort and relieve her shyness of asking a question in public for her problem. In other words, Rasulullah ﷺ acknowledged her by using her child's name to show that Rasulullah ﷺ knows her and that is normal to ask about a problem. If one reviews other narrations about Rasulullah ﷺ, there are many instances that people come and ask for their problems and Rasulullah ﷺ immediately gives them attention and answers their problem. Rasulullah ﷺ had the utmost sense of fulfilling the responsibility of the prophethood and messengership from Allah سبحانه وتعالى. Rasulullah ﷺ often asked people if they would witness for him after death in front of Allah سبحانه وتعالى that Rasulullah ﷺ had fulfilled this difficult responsibility of messengership of Allah سبحانه وتعالى.

8. Abu Hurayra narrates that one day a desert man who doesn't know the etiquettes of social and civil life came to Rasulullah ﷺ. Rasulullah ﷺ was sitting in the mosque. The man started praying in the mosque and said loudly in the mosque in his prayer: "Oh Allah! Have mercy only on me and only on Muhammad. Don't be merciful on anyone except us." Rasulullah ﷺ called the man next to him and said: "Do you think you can limit the Mercy of Allah سبحانه وتعالى?" Then, the man left and started urinating inside the mosque. The people in the mosque saw this and got very angry and ran towards the man. Rasulullah ﷺ stopped the people doing harm to the man and said to the people: "You are given the responsibility of being facilitators to make it easy for people. You are not charged with being aggravators and making situations worse. Pour a bucket of water over the urine and let it go [6] [1] [4] [9] [2] (285)."

Commentary

Rasulullah ﷺ was always kind and considerate but not harsh. In the cases of situations where a person can be easily angry, Rasulullah ﷺ was always tempered with forbearance and patience. Rasulullah ﷺ had empathy for the people with their different levels of education, cultural and ethnic backgrounds. In another narration of the above case, Rasulullah ﷺ told the people who were rushing to stop the man urinating in the mosque, said: "Let the man finish his need and tell him nicely that it is wrong to do it in the mosque." Rasulullah ﷺ did not want people to stop the man in the middle of his urination due to this human need of discharge in case he gets sick. After, they can teach him nicely that there are places of human discharge such as restrooms but not in the prayer places or any other places of human social venues.

9. Nawwas bin Sima'n said " I asked one day to Rasulullah ﷺ, what is virtue and evil?" Rasulullah ﷺ replied: "Virtue is an ethical and kind behavior. Evil is what you hide in your heart and you dislike people to know about" [2] (2553).

Commentary

The virtue is described by Rasulullah ﷺ as a type of disposition and behavior of ethics, morality and kindness. Oppositely, when there is a disposition or a behavior that the person can be embarrassed about and looked down upon when it is known by others, this can be possibly an evil or vice.

10. Oppression is the darkness on the Day of Resurrection [2] (2579).

Commentary

According to the above testimony of Rasulullah ﷺ, the oppression and evil renderings of a person in this world will be darkness in the afterlife. The darkness can symbolize the accountability and punishment of the person due to this evil. One of the greatest oppressions is the person's unrecognition and unappreciative behavior towards Allah سبحانه وتعالى although Allah سبحانه وتعالى created the person and gave them their livelihood. In this perspective, a believer and one appreciative of Allah سبحانه وتعالى will have a light.

11. All the believers are like one single person. If this person's eye hurts, then all the body has uneasiness and pain due to this. If this person has a headache, this person's entire body carries the pain and is in discomfort, [2] (2586R3).

Commentary

The above testimony of Rasulullah ﷺ establishes a social solidarity among all believers and humans. The suggested social solidarity in the above statement is standing together against oppression, evil and human problems. In a practical sense, if people are dying of hunger in one part of the world, a believer of Allah سبحانه وتعالى, a Muslim cannot say "I don't care." According to the above narration, one should feel the pain and suffering of others even if the person cannot do anything about it.

12. When two people are involved in abuses, it will be the first one who start the abuse be the sinner as long as the second does not oppress the other in retribution [2] (2587).

Commentary

According to the above narration, although it is a higher status to forgive one another according to the teachings of the Quran and the Prophet Muhammad ﷺ, an abused person has the right to counter back the abuse. In this case of retribution, it is critical not to transgress the limits of payback because the person now can become an abuser although he or she did not initiate the abuse. The justice, ethics and morality should be observed in all different cases of life encounters if one is the weak or strong.

13. Charity does not decrease the wealth. Allah ﷻ increases the respect of the one who forgives others. Allah ﷻ elevates the person who shows humbleness for the sake of Allah ﷻ [2] (2588).

Commentary

In the above testimony of Rasulullah ﷺ, Allah ﷻ gives respect to the person when someone abused this person through any means. In the Islamic tradition as mentioned in the previous narration, the person has the right to take back what is due to on one without going over limits.

In the case of forgiving but not executing the due process, Allah ﷻ gives respect to this person in social and kinship disputes.

The other part of the narration alludes to the virtue of humbleness compared to arrogance. Allah ﷻ elevates this person similarly in the society and in one's relationship with Allah ﷻ when this person adopts humbleness as a trait. Lastly, the above testimony also has the encouragement to give charity and help the people in need. Although one can think causatively of decrease in wealth in the habit of giving, Allah ﷻ assures that there will be a blessing and abundance but not decrease in one's habit of giving charity for a good cause with a good intention.

14. Do you know what is backbiting? The people around Rasulullah ﷺ replied: "Allah ﷻ and Messenger of Allah ﷺ knows the best. "Then, Rasulullah ﷺ said: To mention something disliked about your brother or sister in their absence. Then, the people around Rasulullah ﷺ asked: "even if it was really the case and the truth about this person?" Then, Rasulullah ﷺ replied: "if what is mentioned is really true about this person, then this is backbiting. If it is not true, then it is slander." [2] (2589).

Commentary

According to the above testimony of Rasulullah ﷺ, one can define the notions of backbiting and slander in Islam. Backbiting is a disliked but a true statement about someone in their absence. Slander is a disliked but a false statement about someone in their absence. In Islamic legal rulings, slander is a greater offense and sin than backbiting. In Islamic sermons, there are numerous references to this statement of Rasulullah ﷺ in order to prevent backbiting and slandering and establish social and kinship solidarity and unity. One should remember that backbiting in Islamic discourses are these statements about others for no purpose during chatting and conversations. If there is a purpose of mentioning someone's disliked trait for a purpose for example in consultations of business, marriage and commitment attempts, then it is not called backbiting but it is considered as a careful, honest and sincere expression of an advice to prevent an evil outcome. Therefore, it is a critical urge and call to check one's intentions when talking unpleasantly about others. In addition, backbiting in Islam does not only include verbal discourses but facial expressions to imply unpleasant things about others can be included in the category of backbiting.

---

15. If a person conceals the faults of another fellow in this world then, Allah ﷻ conceals this person's faults in the Day of Judgment [2] (2590R1).

Commentary

According to the above testimony of Rasulullah ﷺ, it is very important not to expose faults of others. One of the Names of Allah ﷻ in Islam is the Concealer. Allah ﷻ does not expose our evil renderings in this world although Allah ﷻ knows, sees and watches everything. Similarly, if the person does not expose people's faults then, Allah ﷻ will not expose the fault of this person in the Day of Judgement where everyone's faults will be exposed and accounted for. The above faults are personal renderings which do not affect others but only the person him or herself. If there are cases where the rights of others are violated and there is an abuse and transgression, the person is encouraged not to hide it but seek solutions to stop the evil.

---

16. If a person is devoid of kindness, then he or she is devoid of good, ethics and morality [2] (2592).

Commentary

Rasulullah ﷺ emphasizes the notion of positive, kind and gentle attitude before any action. In other words, the way of delivery of the message, social communications, conversations, and any daily discourses should entail kindness but not harshness. To prove this point, one of the verses in the Quran [2:263] mentions this very clearly that if one is going to give charity in a harsh or arrogant attitude, it is better for this person not to give any monetary help to others but first to be nice, gentle and kind in verbal discourse. In other words, the best way is to give charity with an attitude of humbleness and kindness. Allah ﷻ appreciates the state of the heart and the attitude of caring and kindness towards others not the outcomes or achievements usually applauded by humans.

17. The worst of the people is the one who is the double-faced. This person approaches some with one face and others with another face [2] (2526R2).

Commentary

Rasulullah ﷺ instructs people to be upright with their intention and action. Sometimes, people leave or oppose the ethical and moral values that they feel in their conscience to be true. Due to their fear or other personal interest, they may change their true disposition. In this sense, a purposeful change or not genuine stance can be also in this category.

18. A believer with good character can attain to the spiritual status of a person who attained it with piety and worship of fasting and praying at nights (4798) [1].

Commentary

The above is a very interesting statement of Rasulullah ﷺ for our times. On one side, there is the piety struggle of a person through prayers and fasting to attain closeness to Allah ﷻ. On another side, there is a person of good moral and ethical character. They can both attain closeness to Allah ﷻ through different paths. In both conditions, the only common requirement is the initial step of recognition and appreciation of Allah ﷻ.

19. Humans are mines like mines of silver and gold. The best of you in character before Islam is the best of you in Islam if they have an understanding [2] (2638R1).

Commentary

According to the above testimony of Rasulullah ﷺ, the characters of people are similar to the valuables of gold or silver. Sometimes, there is a question asked among some people that if someone is ethical why he or she needs to be religious or believe in Allah ﷻ. According to this narration, a person who has good ethical and moral sound qualities such as honesty, trustworthiness, appreciation, or gratitude etc. has more potential to excel after becoming Muslim. In other words, one of the goals of the religion in Islam is to enable people to have good ethical and moral traits and characters with other humans, with all the creation and Allah ﷻ. Having good character in one's relationship with Allah ﷻ includes recognition of all the bounties from One and Only God and appreciating all with gratitude. The person embodying this essence is called Muslim. The phrase "if they have an understanding" can signify that the person should maintain the traits of good character after becoming Muslim in accordance with the teachings of the Quran and Rasulullah ﷺ. In other words, in one's new life of being a Muslim, one should always check and balance this innate good character with the guidelines of the religion.

20. A believer of Allah ﷻ is not fulfilled from doing good action until he or she enters Heaven [4] (2686).

Commentary

Above is a testimony of Rasulullah ﷺ that a person who appreciates and believes in Allah ﷻ does not stop doing good until he or she dies. Then, due to his or her belief in Allah ﷻ and having spent their lives in doing good, ethical and moral, Allah ﷻ places this person in Heaven.

21. If a person relieves another person (a believer), from the difficulties and burdens of life, then Allah ﷻ relieves this person from the difficulties of life after death, [2] (2699).

Commentary

In Islam, a person can transform performing regular ethical and moral duties for other humans as a pious religious act. Sometimes a person may not give importance to ease someone's difficulties. However, this can be a means for this person to go to Heaven in afterlife as mentioned above. In addition, Allah ﷻ teaches humans to have social solidarity by having empathy with the ones who are in difficulty.

22. When a person is easy on a hard-pressed person then, Allah ﷻ will be easy on him or her in this life and life after death [2] (2699).

Commentary

One can witness a lot of people who are oppressed, hard-pressed or experiencing calamities and troubles. In the above testimony of Rasulullah ﷺ from Allah ﷻ, when a person encounters such people if the person takes the stance of being easy, nice and kind to them compared others then, Allah ﷻ will make the things easy for this person in this world and after death. Sometimes, we tend to follow the trends what people or culture dictate for us in the expectation of social, professional and familial relationships. According to this narration of Rasulullah ﷺ, if a person takes a moment to ponder about one's stance in a common treatment of others, one can transform this opportunity as means of pleasing Allah ﷻ and possibly pleasing and helping to this hard-pressed person. For example, if a person is under financial bankruptcy and going through some crisis, although it may be difficult, a loan owner can forgive some or all of the debt in order to make it easy for this hard-pressed person.

23. Whoever covers the fault of a person (believer) Allah ﷻ will cover his or her faults in this life and life after death [2] (2699).

Commentary

According to the above testimony of Rasulullah ﷺ, it is important not to publicize the faults of a person if it is not endangering others. Especially, talking about private life of others, gossiping, making fun of them, and back biting are some of these categories that a person should not publicize the faults of others. In other words, acting with wisdom for correcting someone is always the suggested and practiced methodology of the Prophet Muhammad ﷺ. There were incidents that when people came to Rasulullah ﷺ to disclose their sins Rasulullah ﷺ told them not to disclose it but to ask forgiveness from Allah ﷻ. In this perspective disclosing one's sins to others and others listening and publicizing them are not virtuous traits in Islam because Allah ﷻ is the Most Forgiving and Concealer of the sins.

24. One day a man came to Rasulullah ﷺ. Then, he said: "Oh Messenger of Allah! I had an illicit relationship with a woman in private outside the city but not fornication. Here I am! please apply whatever you need to apply. "Omar was there also and said to the man "Allah ﷻ concealed your fault. You better not reveal your sin!" Rasulullah ﷺ, however, was silent, did not give any response and kept his silence. Then, the man stood up and left. Rasulullah ﷺ sent another person to call him back and then, Rasulullah ﷺ recited to this man a new revelation of the Quran about this case as "And be constant in praying at the beginning and the end of the day, as well as during the early watches of the night: for, verily, good deeds drive away evil deeds: this is a reminder to all who bear [God] in mind.[22] [14]" Then, the man said : "Oh messenger of Allah ﷻ, is this new revelation of Quran only for me?" Rasulullah ﷺ said: "no, for everyone." [2] (2763R3).

---

22. [11,114]

In the above report, there are a few important points to analyze. First, there was a sharp change in the prior value system of people in few years with the advent of new values of Islam. One of the value systems that were immensely engraved especially in the early companions was the understanding of accountability in front of Allah ﷻ. In the above case, even though a possible offense was done in privacy, this person still wanted to receive retribution for his action. This was possibly due to the embodiment of the notion that although people did not witness his engagement but Allah ﷻ witnessed it. This concept was especially vivid and practiced in the early Muslims who were living at the time of Rasulullah ﷺ with Rasulullah ﷺ. People wanted to pay back for the offense that they did which harmed their relation with Allah ﷻ. Some may refer to this as the internal conscience or awareness of God in their life so vivid that the pain of guilt overpowered the possible pain of punishment.

The second point is about the ethics of early companions. In this situation, Omar, a prominent Muslim companion of Rasulullah ﷺ immediately urged the man not to disclose his fault in public and keep it between him and Allah ﷻ. In Islam, God can forgive all the sins as long as the person recognizes One and Only Creator. The early Muslims' ethics of hiding the fault of others can also be observed in the field of transmission of the hadith, the sayings and practices of Rasulullah ﷺ. For example, when there was a disliked action or fault, the early companions or narrators did not mention their name. In this narration for example, it narrates as "a man came to Rasulullah ﷺ," then it explains the narration. If it was something good one can find the name of the person in the narrations.

Another point is the stance of Rasulullah ﷺ that he did not instruct people about the religious teachings according to his own idea or judgment unless there was an instruction or revelation from Allah ﷻ about the situation. In this case, Rasulullah ﷺ kept silent and did not respond to the man until he received revelation from Allah ﷻ.

This report also shows a difference between the Quran and Torah. The Quran was revealed in pieces in 23 years, was contextualized according to the time, place and people[23]. From this contextualization, it was then generalized so that one can deduce and analyze meanings for similar cases as mentioned in the last portion of above testimony of Rasulullah ﷺ.

Lastly, according to the Islamic teachings, God gives numerous opportunities to a person in life to be forgiven by doing good deeds. In this case, one can see that five times daily prayers wipes off the offenses or sins performed between each prayer intervals. Therefore, it is suggested after each bad rendering that one should precede with a good action in order to compensate for the possible offense. One of the good actions is the remembrance of Allah ﷻ through regular and five times a day prayers in Islam.

---

23. called sabab nuzul in its technical term.

Christians, Jews, and Non-Muslims

Three groups have double reward. One of them is a person from the people of the scripture believing in their Prophet and believing Muhammad as the messenger of Allah [6] [2] ﷺ.

1. Three groups have double rewards. One of them is a person from the people of the scripture believing in their Prophet and believing Muhammad as the messenger of Allah ﷺ [6] [2].

Commentary

When a Christian believes in Jesus (Isa) عليه السلام or a Jew who believes in Moses (Musa) عليه السلام and at the same time if this person believes in Muhammad as the prophet of Allah ﷺ, then this person has double rewards from Allah ﷺ in Islam teachings. It could be difficult sometimes for people to recognize a genuine or true teaching due to the hindrance of group identities. Therefore, going beyond these group identities and realizing the similarities of the messages is an achievement. Therefore, it can be due to this difficult identity struggle of the person that the person receives a double reward compared to a person who could be born in a Muslim family.

2. When the people of Book, the Christians, or Jews narrate you any parts from Bible: the Gospel, the Psalms, and the Torah, from their books, neither confirm them nor deny them, and be in neutral state and say to them:

> "We believed in Allah ﷺ, we believed whatever book Allah ﷺ revealed, the Bible: the Gospel, the Psalms, and the Torah, and we believed in the teachings of the messengers such as Abraham (Ibrahim), Moses (Musa) & Jesus (Isa) عليهم السلام and others."

When you do like this, you don't deny them if they are really the truth from the original Bible: the Gospel, the Psalms, and the Torah, the true teachings of their Prophets and you don't accept if they are false or fabricated [1] (12) and [10] (4/136).

Commentary

Islam is not a new religion but the continuation of the original message of Abraham (Ibrahim), as Moses (Musa) & Jesus (Isa) عليهم السلام, and other prophets and messengers of Allah. The creed of Islam is worshipping one God alone and not involving any associates with God implicitly or explicitly. In other words, Islam came to Prophet Muhammad in Arabia in 610 CE just to revive and reinstate the original message sent to Abraham (Ibrahim), Moses (Musa) & Jesus (Isa) عليهم السلام, and other messengers sent by Allah at different times in human history but their names are not mentioned.

Muslims are required to believe in all the books that were revealed by Allah. In the creed system of Islam, a Muslim is required to believe in the Quran, Bible: The Gospels, Psalms, and Torah, and all other communications sent by Allah. According to the above narration, Rasulullah teaches Muslims that they need to make a distinction that they believe in the authentic versions of these sacred books and teachings of the prophets.

---

3. I was sent as a messenger and a prophet by Allah for all humans [6] (tay. 1) & [10] (3/304)

Commentary

According to the Islamic theology, God sent at different times of history different prophets and messengers to different groups and nations living in certain specific areas. The message of all these prophets and messengers were the same. For example, recognizing one Creator, worshipping Allah, and being accountable in this world and afterlife. Unlike the Prophet Muhammad, he was sent as the last messenger of Allah to humans and he was sent to all humans instead of one specific area at a specific time. The Prophet has brought the same message similar to the messages of the prior messengers of Allah ﷻ. Until the End of Day, there won't be any other messenger. Therefore, regardless of a person accepting the Prophet Muhammad ﷺ as his or her prophet, when a person dies at our contemporary time until the End of Day, immediately, there will be three questions asked in the grave of this person by the angels: 1) Who is your Creator? 2) Who is your Prophet? 3) How did you spend your time?

The expected answers would be Allah ﷻ for question one and the Prophet Muhammad ﷺ for the second one. The person will not be able to answer these questions unless one recognized, accepted and internalized these answers in their lifetime. It is interesting to note that Muslims believe that Jesus (Isa) عليه السلام will come before the End of Day to correct the mischief on the earth and to bring peace to all world. His position at this time will not be bringing his religion but following the Prophet Muhammad ﷺ as one of the followers. Muslims believe that all the prophets Muhammad, Abraham (Ibrahim), Moses (Musa) and Jesus (Isa) عليهم السلام, or other messengers sent by Allah ﷻ bringing the same essential message from Allah ﷻ. Therefore, prophets are like brothers of the same family there is no competition of group identity or religion as long as everyone serves as a vehicle to bring the recognition and appreciation of Allah ﷻ and establish ethics and justice on the earth.

---

4. Me and the similitude of other Prophets and Messengers of Allah ﷻ such as Abraham (Ibrahim), Moses (Musa) and Jesus (Isa) عليهم السلام, and others is like this:
    A person builds a nice building. Everyone comes and visits this building says: We have never seen a building more beautiful and perfect than this one except one missing brick that we see.

    Then, Rasulullah ﷺ says: I am this brick.

Commentary

The Prophet Muhammad is the last messenger of Allah ﷻ among others, to complete the jigsaw puzzle if one can describe as according to the above narration. Therefore, through the teachings of the Prophet Muhammad ﷺ and the Quran, one can find meaning, respect and elevation of the status of other prophets such as Abraham (Ibrahim), Moses (Musa) and Jesus (Isa) عليهم السلام and other books such as the Bible: the Gospel, the Psalms, and the Torah. In that regard, the teachings of the Prophet Muhammad ﷺ, Islam, is complimentary, and universal and giving inclusive meaning for the other messengers and scriptures of Allah ﷻ.

One should also note that the Prophets and messengers of Allah ﷻ are role models and chosen by Allah ﷻ[24]. They are humans and they can make mistakes but they are protected from major, unethical and evil sins by Allah ﷻ. Therefore, the biblical understanding of Prophets with Islam is different. Therefore, there are similarities in biblical stories about the Prophets but there are also differences. Some of the biblical stories showing and depicting some of the messengers and prophets of Allah ﷻ involving in evil and unethical behavior as a human venture is considered false and fabricated in Islamic scholarship. Islamic theology through the Quran and sayings of Rasulullah ﷺ explain that in the original versions of these divine scriptures these versions of the stories did not exist but added and the original ones altered over time.

---

5. Allah ﷻ created Adam as a manifestation and image of the Divine Attributes [6] (6227).

Commentary

It is interesting to note that the above saying of Rasulullah ﷺ is also mentioned similarly in the Bible [16]. In Muslim interpretation of the above saying is that the word "image" is not taken literally but figuratively. In that sense, humans can set a goal in their spiritual and ethical journey in order to manifest different attributes of Allah ﷻ in a tiny scale on the earth. For example, a person can give charity and be called generous. The real source of generosity is Allah ﷻ, the Most Generous.

---

24. This is known as the "ismah," about the messengers and prophets of God. This is defined as the condition of being protected from the major sins with the Grace and Mercy of God.

6. Ibn Abbas narrates that the Christians and Jews used to let their
   hair fall on their head and the people who did not purely believe
   in Allah ﷻ used to part their hair as the sign of their identities.
   The Prophet liked to act similar to the Christians and Jews as the
   believers of Allah ﷻ unless there was a revelation from Allah ﷻ.
   Therefore, Rasulullah ﷺ initially made the style of his hair like the
   Christians and Jews and later in his lifetime, Rasulullah ﷺ made
   his hairstyle, parting them like others [2].

Commentary

The Prophet fully recognized the Christians and Jews as the followers of
Allah ﷻ that the Muslims also believe in follow. Therefore, in the matters
of identity, if there was no revelation from Allah ﷻ, Rasulullah ﷺ took
the position of being similar to the Christians and Jews. Later, as in the
above case, the matter of the hair style as an identity could have been
changed either due to the instruction of a divine revelation or due to a
change in cultural and identity norms of that society in practice. Then,
Rasulullah ﷺ did not have problem making his hair style similar to
others [2] (2336).

7. One day, someone said to Rasulullah ﷺ: "Curse on the polytheists,
   non-Muslims!" The Prophet replied: "I was not sent by Allah ﷻ to
   curse people. Indeed, and definitely, I was sent to all mankind by
   Allah ﷻ as a merciful, caring, kind and loving person." [2] (2599).

Commentary

One can see the values of a pre-Islamic society with strong discriminatory
identity traits of religion, ethnicity, wealth and gender. The Prophet
meticulously worked to establish a new society with completely new
values in his prophetic mission of 23 years. There are a lot of historical
incidents as well as the Quranic passages that would applaud the
pleasing kind and gentle character of Rasulullah ﷺ while striving to
change these harsh embedded discriminatory traits in individuals. The

above is an example that Rasulullah ﷺ instructs the Muslims not to discriminate and treat people harshly because they are not Muslims, even if they may not believe in God.

---

8. Do not choose and select among the prophets and messengers of Allah ﷻ [1] (4668).

Commentary

In the above testimony of Rasulullah ﷺ, Rasulullah ﷺ emphasizes not to get into to the useless and futile arguments with Muslims, Christians and Jews for the identity superiority of the prophets and messengers of God. In Islam, God sent all the prophets and messengers with the same message. This is the essence. Different prophets and messengers were sent to remind the same message from God and reinstate the original teachings sent by God. In this perspective in Islam, a Muslim is not an identity tag for only followers of the Prophet Muhammad ﷺ, but it is also used for the true followers of Abraham (Ibrahim), Moses (Musa) and Jesus (Isa) عليهم السلام, Abraham and others when they follow the correct and authentic message from God.

Jesus (Isa) عليه السلام

> *All the prophets have different mothers but the same*
> *father. Jesus (Isa) عليه السلام is my brother. There is no*
> *other prophet between me and him. I am the closest one*
> *to Jesus [3] [1] [2] (2365).*

1. All the prophets have different mothers but the same father. Jesus
   (Isa) is my brother. There is no other prophet between me and
   him. I am the closest one to Jesus (Isa) [6] [1] [2] (2365).

Commentary

The Prophet Muhammad mentions that he is the true and last Prophet of
Allah ﷻ sent by Allah ﷻ after Jesus (Isa) عليه السلام. Therefore, Rasulullah
ﷺ emphasizes a special type of affinity and relation with Jesus (Isa)
عليه السلام due to this uninterrupted and successive position of his
messengership. There was no true or authentic prophet and messenger
officially sent by Allah ﷻ to humans except Rasulullah ﷺ Muhammad
after the Prophet Jesus (Isa) عليه السلام.

It can be also implied that the Prophet Abraham has the title of the
father of Prophets. Some of the scholars interpret above narration of
having the same father and different mother as follows. Having the same
father can mean that all the prophets in essence bring the same message
of believing One and Only, Unique Creator. The Prophet Abraham was
known to be the symbol of this message. On the other hand, having
different mothers can mean figuratively that the religions can be
different if not in their essence but in their secondary applications. For
example, in one religion, the day of temple visit can be Sunday, on the
other it can be on Saturday or Friday. In major ethics codes for example,
Allah سبحانه وتعالى has always ordered the same teachings for all humans
through prophets in the course of history. For example, taking the life of
an innocent being is considered a grave sin across the religions which is
same and common in the essence of all these religions.

There are striking similarities between the Prophet Jesus (Isa) عليه السلام and the Prophet Muhammad ﷺ. Both of them did not have a real exposure of a father. The Prophet Jesus (Isa) عليه السلام did not have a father. The father of Prophet Muhammad passed away before he was born. The Prophet Muhammad was raised as an orphan. Both of them received a Divine Message from Allah سبحانه وتعالى, the Gospel and the Quran.

Both were supported by Ruhul Qudus. It is interesting to note that the literal translation of this term is the Holy Spirit. The support of Ruhul Qudus is mentioned for both of the Prophets Jesus (Isa) عليه السلام and Muhammad ﷺ. In most of the Islamic interpretations, the Ruhul Qudus was arc angel Gabriel who brought revelation and who actually came in human form to interact.

Finally, one of the utmost similarities between the two is their characters. They had both predominant quality and characters of gentleness, mercy, calmness and peace for all creation.

---

2. All the children of Adam are touched by Satan at the day when their mother gave birth to them except Virgin Mary and her son, Jesus [2] (2366).

Commentary

The above testimony is from the Prophet Muhammad ﷺ about Virgin Mary and the Prophet Jesus (Isa) عليه السلام. Allah سبحانه وتعالى has protected both Virgin Mary and Jesus exceptionally due to possibly their false expected blames and slanders for the birth of the Prophet Jesus. In other words, Allah سبحانه وتعالى protected them in such an extent as in the above narration that there is no room of slandering such as adultery and so forth for the incident of miraculous birth of Jesus enabled by Allah سبحانه وتعالى.

On the other hand, the Prophet Jesus was the true messenger of Allah سبحانه وتعالى and that there is no involvement of lies and untruths about the divine message that he brought from Allah سبحانه وتعالى. Even, at his birth, he was protected from any type of false renderings from Satan.

Still, some people did not believe his message and continued with their own biased arguments. Touched by Satan can be a figurative rendering of the mission of Satan which is to distract the humans from their real purpose of their presence on earth.

The concept of original sin does not exist in Islam. Everyone acquires their good or bad deeds starting from the age of puberty and maturation. A baby or a child does not have an ability to differentiate what is wrong or right until they reach to an age of reason. This concept is similar in both Islam and Judaism.

---

3.   One day, Jesus, the son of Maryam saw a man stealing. Then, he said to him: Did you steal? The man replied: No, never. I swear on the One that there is no deity except God. Then, Jesus said: I have believed in Allah سبحانه وتعالى and my own self lied to me [2] (2368).

Commentary

In the above narration, there are a few points. The Prophet Jesus does not blame the man but he blames himself for a possible mistake of his senses of eye sight, thoughts and other humanly encounters. The character of Prophet Jesus as a role model was very fair, lenient and immediately turned to the truth and self-accountability but did not insist on the falsehood.

Some of the Muslim scholars show above narration among many others that Prophet Jesus had mentioned that he was a human and he could have done minor mistakes as a human being. Also, he was the messenger of Allah سبحانه وتعالى like other messengers and prophets of Allah سبحانه وتعالى.

Lastly, the man also swears as "One that there is no deity except God, Allah." The belief in One Allah سبحانه وتعالى has always been the case as a simple, objective and straightforward statement. This is also the declaration of faith in Islam as well called shahada. This shows according to the Muslims the main creed of all religions of Allah سبحانه وتعالى did not change over time. It was always the same.

4. No one talked in their cradle as a baby except three: Jesus, the friend of Jurayj and the suckling baby [2] (2550R1).

Commentary

The above narration of Rasulullah ﷺ mentions the miraculous talking of the three different babies in human history.

The first case was the case of Isa عليه السلام as a baby and infant. Allah سبحانه وتعالى makes him speak as mentioned in detail in the Quran. In the Quranic description, Allah سبحانه وتعالى enables Isa عليه السلام to speak as a miracle in order to defend his mother Maryam in regards to her chastity that Allah سبحانه وتعالى sent Isa عليه السلام as a special messenger with miraculous conception without any father but only a mother, Maryam.

The second case is about a pious man who dedicated his life to worship. One day, his mother called him constantly and he was engaged in his prayer, enjoying it, and did not want to disturb his prayer. His mom then was upset with her son and made a prayer to Allah سبحانه وتعالى against him saying "Oh Allah! here is my son, I am calling him and he is not responding. Give a tribulation and difficulty to him!" After this incident, Jurayj, the very pious man was slandered to fornicate and a child was born with wedlock. As the people were very angry to Jurayj who was known to be pious in town, he prayed to Allah سبحانه وتعالى and put his hand on the baby's body and said "who is your father?" Allah سبحانه وتعالى made the baby speak miraculously and the baby denied Jurayj as his father.

The last one was about a suckling baby with his mother. While the baby was suckling, the mother saw a nice looking rich man walking outside on the street. The mother said: "oh Allah! make my son like this man." Then, Allah سبحانه وتعالى made the baby speak: "Oh Allah! don't make me like him." Later, a poor girl was passing on the street and people were beating her due to an accusation of theft and adultery about her. The mother said: "Oh Allah! don't make my baby like her." Then, the baby said: "Oh Allah! make me like her." Then, the mother got angry and said to her baby: "Oh bald head! there was a nice rich man and I made prayer to Allah سبحانه وتعالى for you to be like him and you opposed my prayer.

Then, there was a bad girl and I made prayer to Allah سبحانه وتعالى for you not to be like her and you opposed my prayer. The baby said: "the man was arrogant and tyrannical. The girl was innocent, ethical and pious."

As one can see in all the three cases, Allah سبحانه وتعالى makes the babies speak against slander. In all cases interestingly, there are the presence of mothers in all of the incidents.

5. Do not select and choose among the Prophets and Messengers of God [1] (4668).

Commentary

Above is the testimony of the Prophet Muhammad ﷺ. The followers of different religions such as Muslims, Christians, or Jews should not be in superiority identity arguments about the messengers or prophets of Allah سبحانه وتعالى. Allah سبحانه وتعالى sent them all with the same message and mission to humans.

Social Conflicts & Violence

It is not permissible for a believer to cut ties and not to talk with one's brother or sister more than three days. When they happen to meet with each other one wants to avoid in order not to talk but the best one among them is the one who initiates the talk and greeting of peace [2] (2560).

1. (the Narrator says: Rasulullah ﷺ offered prayer for the deceased of the Uhud and climbed up to the pulpit as if it was his farewell for all, living and non-living) I will be waiting for you in the special pool, Hawd, in Heaven for you. This pool is so big and wide similar to the distance between Aila and Juhfa. After I die, I am not afraid that you would worship anything except Allah ﷻ. But, I am afraid about the false attractions of the world for you, competing with each other about it, killing each other, and therefore, being wiped out and destroyed similar to the people before you. (The narrator says, this was the last time I saw the prophet on the pulpit) [2] (2296R2).

Commentary

The Prophet was informed by Allah ﷻ in his life time about his departure time from the world, about his death. Before he passed away, he was preparing the people about this human reality as Rasulullah ﷺ was a human that he would also die. He was reminding all the Muslims about the general guidelines of Islam. The Prophet stated some prophecies about the future by mentioning what would happen after his death. According to the Islamic scholars [17], the Muslims should take heed from the teachings of Rasulullah ﷺ and refrain from the social conflicts and violence. Social conflicts and violence are the destruction of the religion, and the peace, Islam. In the Prophetic teachings, one can clearly realize that teachings of Islam can exist and be practiced in peaceful societies. Individuals cannot live the teachings of their religion in social conflicts and violence.

2. Abu Huraira reported that there were two people arguing in the marketplace about a monetary dispute: a man from the Jews and a man from the Muslims. The Muslim said and swore on the high status of the Prophet Muhammad ﷺ and said "The One who chose Muhammad over all the worlds." Then, the Jew said and swore on the high status of the Prophet Moses and said "The One who chose Moses over all the worlds." Then, the Muslim lifted his hand and slapped the Jew. The Jew went to the Prophet Muhammad ﷺ and told him what happened between him and the Muslim. Then, Rasulullah ﷺ said: "Do not identify me better than Moses. When the people will be resurrected after death, I will be the first human resurrected and I would see Moses already resurrected and holding at the Dominion of Allah ﷻ. I do not know if he was resurrected before me or Allah ﷻ made an exception for him."

3. In a similar narration of the above case, the prophet got very angry and disturbed when he was reported about the incident what the Muslim did to the Jew [2] (2373).

Commentary

One can realize that the instances that Rasulullah ﷺ got angry were very rare. In the above case of the unnecessary identity argument, Rasulullah ﷺ got angry at the Muslim. The Prophet did not approve the identity related fights, arguments, disputes or wars depending on religious superiority. In Islam, everyone's accountability is with Allah ﷻ. In Islamic theology, the messengers of God such as Adam, Noah, Abraham, Moses, Jesus, and Muhammad عليهم السلام are higher ranking Prophets and messengers of Allah ﷻ in their closeness to Allah ﷻ. As the Prophet Muhammad ﷺ has brought the last message, and book from Allah ﷻ, it has the final and updated and the most inclusive message until the End of Days. In that perspective and with others, Muslims scholars explain that the Prophet Muhammad ﷺ had the highest status of closeness to Allah ﷻ chosen among all the creations. In addition, some of the scholars explain the above narration as the actual demonstration of the modesty and humbleness of Rasulullah ﷺ with many other instances in his life. In the above narration, Rasulullah ﷺ also mentions that the first person after the End of Days resurrected in front of Allah ﷻ will be the Prophet Muhammad ﷺ. The scholars explain this for different reasons. The Prophet was the last messenger of Allah ﷻ and he will be the one resurrected first. His message was inclusive of all other messengers and scriptures from Allah ﷻ. He is viewed as the lead Prophet and human since the beginning of creation. Therefore, when Rasulullah ﷺ sees Moses (Musa) عليه السلام already resurrected then, he indicates the high status of Moses (Musa) عليه السلام next to Allah ﷻ as well.

---

4. It is not permissible for a believer to cut ties and not to talk with one's brother or sister more than three days. When they happen to meet with each other, one of them wants to avoid in order not to talk. Yet, the best one between them is the one who initiates the talk and greeting of peace [2] (2560).

Commentary

The Prophet wants to establish a social, kinship and familial solidarity and unity by not carrying on grudges, disputes and conflicts among individuals. In our life, we find a lot of people who are not talking with their own parents, children, relatives and friends for years due to a minor or major dispute. Regardless of the size of the dispute, Rasulullah ﷺ instructs not to carry this negative attitude more than three days. The person can be still upset after three days but initiating the talk and taking the first step can hopefully better the ties. In this perspective, Rasulullah ﷺ encourages to be the first person to take the positive first step of forgiveness and moving on. There are other sayings of Rasulullah ﷺ that mentions about the one who first greets first than another would be safe from arrogance in his or her heart. Therefore, in a society when good manners are encouraged by the religion, then it can be an important avenue for reducing our global conflicts and hatred. It is a common practice among the Muslims to remind each other this three-day rule as a way of advice if someone is severing relations with another person more than three days.

5. Jabir bin Abdullah reported that two young men fell into dispute. One was from the group of muhajirun (the immigrants) and the other was the group of ansar (the local residents and supporters). The muhajir boy called his fellows from his group and the ansar called the fellows from his group. Then Rasulullah ﷺ came out and said: "What is this, the teachings of days of ignorance[25]? They said: "Oh Messenger of Allah! There is nothing serious. Two young men fell into dispute and one struck the back of other. The Prophet said: "ok, it is not a problem. The person should help his brother or sister whether he or she is oppressed or oppressor. If he or she is oppressor, then one should prevent this person. If he or she is the oppressed, then one should help this person. [2] (2584).

Commentary

In the above testimony of Rasulullah ﷺ, one can see that Rasulullah ﷺ reminds the early Muslims their lives prior to Islam. In Islamic literature, these days are referred as the days of ignorance, jahilliyyah. Tribal wars, female infanticide, injustice, racism, women oppression, and other practices were norms in that pre-Islamic society. When Rasulullah ﷺ came out to the scene in the above narration, his immediate response was "are you going back to your injustice practices?" by helping each other with tribal, racial or group associations but not on the merits of morality, good, and preventing evil and oppression. The last statement of Rasulullah ﷺ summarizes this teaching about the notion of helping both the oppressor and oppressed. This teaching has been historically interpreted, practiced and contemporized differently.

6. Should I tell you what is slandering or tale carrying? It is relating and carrying words from one to another which makes people hate and separate from each other. The person continues to tell the truth until the person is given the title of "the truthful." The person continues to tell people lies until the person is given the title of "the liar" [2] (2607).

---

25. Jahilliya in ar.

Commentary

Above is a testimony of Rasulullah ﷺ about the evil engagements of relating conversations from one person or group to another. In the Quranic passages, this notion is very much covered to allude to the types of people who would work purposefully for making chaos, separation, hate, disputes and wars among people through engagement of lies. In other words, these people try to ignite clashes by carrying statements verbal or written among different individuals, groups or communities. As Allah ﷻ is watching everything, there will be accountability for everyone including the liars and the truthful ones in the world and afterlife. Therefore, the titles are already given to people either as the truthful or the liar in a dimension that only Allah ﷻ knows. This reality about their own selves will be revealed to them as soon as one dies and meets with Allah ﷻ.

---

7. When one of you physically fight with another person, then the person should avoid hitting the face [2] (2612).

Commentary

The essence Rasulullah ﷺ's message is to establish justice, and peace to remove verbal disputes and physical fights. If the person is forced to defend oneself or cannot control one's anger, there is an additional possible avenue of oppression or evil when the person harms one face. As one can rationalize, the damage in the head area can be permanent compared to other parts of the body. In another narration, Rasulullah ﷺ mentions that Allah ﷻ created human's in the Divine image. This is not taken literally but a limited hearing, seeing and understanding is given to humans by Allah ﷻ. Allah ﷻ is in essence All-Hearing, All-Seeing and All-Knowing. In this perspective, it is considered respect to Allah ﷻ by respecting humans, especially with their different appearances of faces or bodies without any dislike and harm.

8. Hisham b. Hakim encountered some people detained in Hums. He said to the ruler: "What is this? I heard Rasulullah ﷺ said: "God will torture those who torture people in the world." [2] (2613R3).

Commentary

When there are people imprisoned for any reason, Rasulullah ﷺ instructs not to torture and treat them badly. In that case, Allah ﷻ, the All Seeing and All Powerful will recompense for this abused, mistreated and assaulted person. It is interesting to look the case of inmate/prison system in the early times of Islam during the time of Rasulullah ﷺ. For example, there are incidents that some people were caught while intending to assassinate Rasulullah ﷺ and early Muslims. The Prophet Muhammad did not put them in separate prisons but these people lived with them. The Prophet instructed the Muslims to treat these constricted people fairly with food, clothing and good manners. One can call the early prisoners or constricted people with the word slave as popularized in the West today. These early prisoners or slaves were allowed to be married, have kids and maintain a family life. There was an entire legal system built about this system and numerous books were written about the system of group of these people being adapted in the society or paroled.

One can call this correctional or adjustment of prisoners as slaves in the society with people. After a certain time with the maturity of their level and correctional behaviors, the Quran and the statements of Rasulullah ﷺ encouraged the caretakers to free these prisoners or slaves. One should remember that the early slaves were replacing today's prison system. These prisoners or slaves were not only in one ethnicity or gender but including all. The main source of imprisonment was due to war captives and criminal offenses [18].

Women and Family Life

> *Abu Huraira narrates that one day, a man came to Rasulullah ﷺ and asked him: "Who should I be treating in the best manner in my life?" The Prophet replied: "Your mother. The man continued: "Who is after?" The Prophet replied: "Your mother." The man asked third time: "Who is after?" The Prophet replied: "Your mother." The man continued: "Who is after?" The Prophet replied: "Your father," [2] (2548).*

1. Abu Huraira narrates that one day, a man came to Rasulullah ﷺ and asked him: "Who should I be treating in the best manner in my life?" The Prophet replied: "Your mother." The man continued: "Who is after?" The Prophet replied: "Your mother." The man asked third time: "Who is after?" The Prophet replied: "Your mother." The man continued: "Who is after?" The Prophet replied: "Your father", [2] (2548).

Commentary

The above narration is a very famous one in Muslim practice. It was very shocking to put women over men in a pre-Islamic patriarchal society with pre-Islamic notions. Furthermore, Rasulullah ﷺ Muhammad was giving three times more rights in the treatment of a mother over a father in the kinship relations. In Islamic history, due to this narration and many others, there are a lot of stories about saints and people of God for their genuine treatment of their mothers and fathers [19]. These saints received enormous blessing from Allah ﷻ due to their very kind and gentle treatment of their parents. In the Quran and sayings of the Prophet Muhammad ﷺ, immediately after the rights of God on a person, rights of parents follow and are due [19].

2. The Prophet said to the driver of the camel caravan "drive slowly and gently, there are breakable items, diamonds and pearls in the caravan" [2] (2323).

Commentary

The Prophet advised the driver of the camel caravan to drive the caravan slowly so that the women in the caravan are not disturbed if they were resting or sleeping. The Prophet was using a metaphor and a simile to make similarity of the women like a breakable item. This meant that the women should be treated very gently physically, emotionally and in gender relations. In addition, Rasulullah ﷺ was giving a very high value to the women likening them to diamonds and pearls. The Prophet has many other sayings about women that one should treat them very gently with love and care. These sayings were interesting in a society of harsh desert culture in gender relationships. Therefore, the narrator of the above narration (Abu Qilaba) mentions that if any person in that society had said anything similar to what Rasulullah ﷺ said like the above statement, then they would have been blamed and humiliated about giving value to the women. One can find a lot of narrations or instances that women used to be much more comfortable around Rasulullah ﷺ compared to other prominent early Muslims. The Prophet used to be very gentle, comforting, social and acting with wisdom when interacting with different genders, cultures and age groups.

On another note, the word of "breakable" is also used by Rasulullah ﷺ in a figurative language about women in another narration [20] as "not break or bend the rib, if you do so, then you will break it."

In gender relations, the Prophet Muhammad ﷺ especially emphasizes accepting everyone as they are but not forcing them to change. Especially, Rasulullah ﷺ emphasizes in the above narration the delicate nature of women that they would not tolerate harshness. Some of the scholars interpret that the outcome of divorces or intolerance towards women are due to not understanding this Prophetic teaching properly [20].

3. Whoever likes to have blessing and abundance in one's sustenance and livelihood, and living a long and satisfied life, then he or she should keep the kinship and family relations [2] (2557).

Commentary

There are immense narrations from Rasulullah ﷺ and verses in the Quran about keeping the kinship or family relations or ties good. Even if some of the family members may not visit and may want to cut relations, the person is still expected to keep the relations and keep one's due as required by God. With the observance of this, Allah ﷻ gives a person a blessed and peaceful life with sustenance and livelihood according to the testimony of Rasulullah ﷺ.

4. The wife of Rasulullah ﷺ, Aisha, said: one day, a woman came to my home. She had two daughters. They were in need and they asked if I could help them. I did not have anything except one date. I gave it to her. The mother took the date and split it into two pieces. She gave it to her daughters but she did not eat from it. Then, they got up and left my home. After a while, Rasulullah ﷺ came. I told him the incident. Then, Rasulullah ﷺ said: "The person who is involved with bringing up daughters, and he or she treats them well in their upbringing, then this effort will be a protection for this person from the punishment of hell fire in the afterlife [2] (2629).

Commentary

In the above testimony of Rasulullah ﷺ, there is an encouragement to have daughters, treat them well and enter to Heaven by this means. One should note that Rasulullah ﷺ emphasized and encouraged upbringing girls in a society where the women were overlooked. The Prophet in another narration mentions that in the afterlife, he will be very close and befriend the parents who had daughters and they treated and raised them well [2]. One can also remember that Rasulullah ﷺ had only daughters. All of them were very enamored of their father, the Prophet Muhammad ﷺ.

It is interesting to note that the kinship relationship of the Prophet Muhammad ﷺ with his family was not related with position or royal treatment through wealth. His family did not enjoy a life with luxury. On the contrary, Rasulullah ﷺ preferred to live a life with scarcity and poverty. If Rasulullah ﷺ wanted he could have a very royal, wealthy and luxurious life. Yet, Rasulullah ﷺ preferred the opposite. When Rasulullah ﷺ and his family received any items of wealth or sustenance, they immediately gave it in charity to help the poor.

In the above narration, at one of these times, Rasulullah ﷺ's wife did not have anything to help this poor mother but except with a date. After the death of Rasulullah ﷺ, although the family of Rasulullah ﷺ received stipend and sustenance, they still maintained the similar habits as before during the time of Rasulullah ﷺ.

---

5. Aisha, the wife of Rasulullah ﷺ said: "whoever loves and looks forward to meeting with Allah ﷻ, Allah ﷻ loves to meet with this person. Whoever is not eager to meet with Allah ﷻ, Allah ﷻ is not pleased to meet with this person." Then, I said to Rasulullah ﷺ: "Oh Messenger of Allah! if it is dislike about death, we all have this feeling." Then, Rasulullah ﷺ said: "it is not that, but when a person who has belief, appreciation, and gratitude for Allah ﷻ is given glad tidings of the Mercy, Love and Heaven of Allah ﷻ at the time of death, then this person desires to meet with Allah ﷻ. When a person who does not have belief, appreciation, and gratitude for Allah ﷻ is given the bad news of the accountability and displeasure of Allah ﷻ at the time of death, then this person is not eager to meet with Allah ﷻ [2] (2684).

Commentary

One can see from the above testimony of Rasulullah ﷺ that everyone is going to know their situation in afterlife immediately after death. At this time, depending on the type of the news that the person receives either the person would be eager to meet with Allah ﷻ or not. In addition, as one can understand the life is a trial and test for a person in Islam.

In this perspective, the person immediately receives the result of one's lifelong struggle at the verge of death immediately.

In another perspective, one can see the type of interaction of Rasulullah ﷺ with his wife and other Muslims. There is always the case of learning and teaching. Especially, in this case, the wife of Rasulullah ﷺ, Aisha, immediately enquired without any reservation about something that was not clear for her. It is reported that the wife of Prophet, Aisha, had a very strong and challenging character in her interaction with Rasulullah ﷺ. She did not make any reservations to solve if there were any issues to be raised. Yet, Rasulullah ﷺ always publicly and privately expressed his immense love towards Aisha.

After the demise of Rasulullah ﷺ, as there were some disputes among the Muslims, Aisha had her own disposition about a matter and lead an army herself in order to defend her disposition against the other group. The Prophet's wife, Aisha can be considered as the first commander in chief of an army in Islamic history.

Poverty and Hunger

> *Jabir reports that whenever someone asked about his
> or her need to Rasulullah ﷺ, he never said "no" to any
> person and gave the person whatever he could give or
> more* [2] (2311).

1. Ibn Abbas reports that Rasulullah ﷺ was the most generous of all
   people in giving charity and doing good. Especially, Rasulullah ﷺ
   used to maximize his generosity in the month of fasting, Ramadan.
   The angel Gabriel used to meet every year in Ramadan with
   Rasulullah ﷺ regularly until it ended. The Prophet used to present
   and read the entire Quran to angel Gabriel. As Rasulullah ﷺ used
   to meet with the angel, Rasulullah ﷺ used to be so generous like a
   blowing wind [2] (2308).

Commentary

The Prophet used to be so generous that most of the time, the people
around him needed to interfere and remind him that he had to leave
certain items for his basic needs but he still used to give so much and
reminded people that whatever the person gave for charity to help people
would remain with the person but whatever the person hoarded and
was stingy about would not remain. In other words, he mentioned that
when the person dies only the good deeds such as charity and helping
the poor will be with the person. The person will receive rewards for
them from Allah ﷻ.

As mentioned in the above narration, Rasulullah ﷺ used to receive
revelation through angel Gabriel from Allah ﷻ. The Prophet used to
meet with the angel Gabriel every month of Ramadan in each year
to leave the legacy of the perfect Quran for the immediate and later
generations as Rasulullah ﷺ would be the last prophet and the Quran
would be the last book sent to humans from Allah ﷻ according to the
Islamic creed.

One can also note that for each spiritual encounter coming from Allah 🌸, the person is expected to thank and to be grateful to Allah 🌸. Therefore, Rasulullah 🌸 showed his appreciation to Allah 🌸 due to his meetings with the angel Gabriel. One of ways of showing this appreciation was by being extra generous especially in the month of Ramadan.

Another possible explanation is that as Rasulullah 🌸 suggested everyone to increase one's good deeds in the month of Ramadan, he showed an example by increasing his own charity for the poor in this month.

2.   The Prophet was sleeping in a room outside his home. Omar, one of the early friends of Rasulullah 🌸, entered this room and saw Rasulullah 🌸 sleeping on a simple mat on the ground which made marks on his body. There were a few simple belongings of Rasulullah 🌸 in this room: a pillow filled with date leaves, a small amount of barley, and a small container of water. Looking at the simplicity of the room and Rasulullah 🌸, Omar started crying. The Prophet asked: "Omar, why are you crying?" Omar said: "I can see the marks on your body on one side and on the other side, your simple and humble belongings in the room. I can picture now the kings of Egypt and Persia with their luxuries. They are enjoying the life and you are in hardship." The Prophet said: "Let them take this world and I will have the afterlife." [2]

Commentary

The Prophet lived a very simple and humble life. If he had wanted he could have lived like the kings of other countries as in the narration Omar, the companion of Rasulullah 🌸, was trying to implicitly point out. The Prophet did not want to build castles, mansions or items of luxury for himself but he liked to give and distribute everything to the poor and to the needy. Therefore, the friends and companions of Rasulullah 🌸, seeing this simple life of Rasulullah 🌸, were truly and genuinely touched with Rasulullah 🌸's character with utmost altruism. One should remember that the position of Rasulullah 🌸 was similar to the president of a superpower country at that time. The borders of authority in Muslim states were ranging from Middle East to the parts of Africa. As the ruler of this vast authority, the Prophet Muhammad ﷺ was sleeping on the floor on a simple mat and distributing and giving everything as charity for the needs of others.

---

3. Jabir reports that whenever someone asked about his or her need to Rasulullah ﷺ, he never said "no" to this person and gave the person whatever he could give or more [2] (2311).

Commentary

One of the traits of Rasulullah ﷺ was that he never turned any person in need empty handed. In some cases, it is reported that he even borrowed some items from others to fulfill the needs of the people who were in need.

Animal Rights

There was a woman who was sent for punishment in the afterlife because of her cat. She confined the cat. Neither she fed the cat nor let the cat go out so that the cat can find food for itself but the cat died due to hunger [2] (2619).

1. There was a man traveling by walking on a route. He became so thirsty. Then, he found a water well and went down inside the well and started drinking the water. Then, he climbed up the well. There was a dog around the well. The dog was panting and was trying to lick the moisture around the well due to thirst. Then, the man said to himself "this dog is struck with extreme thirst as I was." Then, the man went down inside the well, filled his shoes with water, held his shoes with his teeth and climbed up the well and gave the water to the dog. Allah ☗ appreciated this man's action and forgave all his sins. Then, the companions, the people around Rasulullah ☗, asked: "Oh Messenger of Allah! Are we also rewarded for our kind treatment of animals?" The Prophet replied: "A reward is granted to the person for helping every living creature" [2] (4280).

Commentary

In another version of the above narration, it was not a man but a prostitute. The woman was traveling in a desert and Allah ☗ forgave her sins due to feeding the thirsty dog. In Islam, one of the core traits is the sincerity of an action. Sincerity is generally defined as doing something only to please Allah ☗ but for no other motive or reason. This disposition makes a very simple minute action very valuable for Allah ☗ [7]. As in the above case, the man did not feed the dog for any reason but as an act of kindness. Thus, for his sincere motive, Allah ☗ forgave all his sins and placed him in Heaven according to the testimony of Rasulullah ☗.

2. A person was sent for punishment to hell due to a cat that she imprisoned and confined. Then, she did not feed the cat with any food. She also did not let it go and release it so that it can eat it from the provisions of the earth. The cat was restrained until it got weak and died, [2] (2619R1).

Commentary

Above is a testimony from Rasulullah ﷺ to allude to the rights of other creations including animals. In the above narration, a person confines a cat and does not feed the cat until the cat dies. As a result, the person is punished for this. In some interpretations of this narration, the above person was known to be a pious person, engaged in the worship of Allah ﷻ. Yet, her piety in its essence also required to respect to other creations of Allah ﷻ including her cat. She did not understand and recognize this. It is also mentioned that Allah ﷻ gives the sustenance of all creation including our contemporary pet animals. Therefore, if this person released the cat as mentioned in the above narration, it would have its provisions from earth. In most of the Muslim countries, one can witness that cats and dogs are freely wandering without any owners among people and without being specifically fed by people [21]. Allah ﷻ gives their provisions by different means.

3. The right of each individual will be paid fully in the Day of Judgment. Even, a sheep without horn will receive its right from the one with horn [2] (2582).

Commentary

One can understand that there is an accountability after death. The accountability will include each person's life engagements in detail. There are some interpretations of the above narration that the animals that were oppressed in life will take their rights from other animals. An example if this is mentioned in the above testimony that a sheep with horn could have oppressed another sheep without horn in their fight or any type of engagement.

The personal relevance of this narration is to encourage the person to live an ethical, just and God conscious life because there will be an accountability after death.

---

4. Imran narrates that one day we were going on a journey in a group with Rasulullah ﷺ. There was a woman who got bored and started cursing to her camel that she was riding on. The Prophet heard this and said: "Please unload your belongings on this animal and set it free because now, it is cursed. The narrator says "I still remember picturing the camel walking with us and no one raised an objection to that [2] (2595).

Commentary

Above is an incident where Rasulullah ﷺ is establishing a respectable environment not only for humans but for animals as well. A person cannot abuse any person or any animal when they are under one's authority. To teach this important rule, Rasulullah ﷺ makes a case against the owner of the animal due to her mistreatment and urges her to set it free.

---

5. There was a woman who was sent for punishment in fire in afterlife because of her cat. She confined the cat. Neither she fed the cat nor let the cat go out so that the cat can find food for itself but the cat died at the end due to hunger [2] (2619).

Commentary

According to the above testimony of Rasulullah ﷺ, when a person is responsible or in charge of anything, anyone, any animal or being, then there is an accountability for this responsibility. In the above case, a person cannot torture an animal or anyone because the person is at a position of being in charge. There is an accountability for everything. In Muslim countries, one can find a lot of pets, animals, cats or dogs wandering freely on the streets unlike to the Western countries where they are domesticated as pets [21]. The portion of the above narration alludes to the fact that Allah ﷻ gives the real sustenance of everything, everyone, and animals. In the above statement, if the person let the cat go, Allah ﷻ would have provided food to it in their natural habitat but the person imprisoned the cat for a long time without any food and the cat died due to hunger.

6. The Prophet narrated that an ant bit one of the messengers. This messenger ordered all the dwelling of the ants to be burnt. Then, Allah ﷻ revealed to this messenger, mentioning "an ant bit you, and you destroyed a nation and species of ants that glorifies, chants and prays to Me? [1] (5266).

Commentary

According to the above testimony of Rasulullah ﷺ, all the ants glorify, chant, and pray to Allah ﷻ. There are clear verses of the Quran that each nation and species of creation chant, glorify and pray to Allah ﷻ except some humans and jinn. In this perspective, no one has the right to kill anything except if there is any harm or application of justice. In the above narration, one can understand one of the main principles in Islamic rulings that a group from the same family of individuals do not bear any responsibility of an individual's crime. In other words, the accountability is at the individual level.

7. Anas narrated that Rasulullah ﷺ has forbidden using animals as a target for arrow shooting [6] [2].

Commentary

Above is a narration that can give some highlight about the change in the society and in social norms before and after the teachings of Rasulullah ﷺ of Islam. While before Islam killing a human did not have much recompense, after the advent of Islam, the regulations guided with divine teachings were applied brought by Rasulullah ﷺ. In the above narration, Rasulullah ﷺ bans people killing animals for the sole purpose of fun, play or game. One should really think about the level of this change with the context of a desert land 1500 years ago. One should not normalize it at our times especially with the advent of values in civilized human societies especially in the last 50 years. The emerging animal rights movements can be example of this advent of values at our times.

Social Life

Do not belittle anything from good, even if it can be a smiling and joyful countenance of your brother or sister [2] (2626).

The one who is not thankful to people will not be thankful to God [1] (4811).

1. Simak asked Jabir: Did you have chance to sit with Rasulullah ﷺ. He said: "Yes, a lot." Then, Jabir explains: The Prophet used to continue to sit with us in the mosque after the morning prayer until sunrise, then after the sunrise, he used to stand up. The friends and companions used to sit next to Rasulullah ﷺ and chat about the silly things that they used to do before Islam and they used to laugh about it. The Prophet was there, listening and he was also smiling" [2] (2322).

Commentary

The Prophet always recognized the humanity of his fellows and engaged with them. Although Rasulullah ﷺ was bringing a serious message from Allah ﷻ about this life and afterlife, Rasulullah ﷺ also did not make people uncomfortable by being cold or not friendly with the mission of Prophethood. There were thousands of people continuously changing their lives significantly. Yet, there were instances in which Rasulullah ﷺ had made jokes as well. However, his jokes were also embedded with wisdom and truth. There were a lot of instances that women and men used to joke around Rasulullah ﷺ comfortably whereas they had a hard time finding the same level of comfort among other prominent early Muslims.

2. Jabir bin Samura narrates that one day, I prayed the first noon prayer[26] with Rasulullah ﷺ. After, Rasulullah ﷺ left to see his family. I walked with him. The Prophet greeted the kids on the street one by one and patted their heads with a smile and Rasulullah ﷺ patted my head as well. I experienced a breeze of cool scent as if his hand was coming from a bottle of perfume [2] (2329).

Commentary

The Prophet is viewed as the father of all Muslims and humans in Islam. The Quran describes Rasulullah ﷺ's mercy towards his people as the one who is merciful, caring and compassionate to all humans. In another passage about the character of Rasulullah ﷺ, he was always concerned about the people. If anything harsh or difficult happens to anyone as the Quran describes, Rasulullah ﷺ was deeply affected due to his deep empathy and altruism similar to the caretaker of everyone. As mentioned, it was one of the habits of Rasulullah ﷺ to engage in dialogue with children and greet them. Therefore, one can find a lot of books in Islamic tradition with the notion of children around Rasulullah ﷺ, taking him as their role model and father.

3. The souls of humans were gathered like an army in the pre-spiritual life before coming to this world. Those who are familiar and know each other will harmonize in this world and the ones who don't know each other can be in disharmony [2] (2638) [6] [1].

Commentary

The understanding of pre-spiritual life[27] is mentioned in the Quran and further explained with the above narration by Rasulullah ﷺ. Accordingly, human souls were created and together in pre-spiritual life before coming to this world. In that world, some of the souls had affinity and acquaintance with each other. Therefore, the experiences of

---

26. Zuhr
27. Qawlu Bala

people when seeing a stranger and immediately feeling very close to that
person is often linked to the affinity of the souls in the pre-spiritual life
in Muslim practice.

4. One day, Rasulullah ﷺ was praying and there were people praying
   behind him. While he was praying, he took off his shoes and put
   at his left side. The people behind him saw this and did exactly
   the same. After Rasulullah ﷺ finished his prayer, he said: "why
   did you took off your shoes?" They replied: "We saw that you
   took off your shoes therefore we took off our shoes as well." Then,
   Rasulullah ﷺ said: "The angel Gabriel came to me during the
   prayer and informed me that there was dirt on my shoes." Then,
   Rasulullah ﷺ continued "when one of you come to the mosque,
   the person should look at one's shoes if the person sees dirt, then
   they can clean it and pray with it" [1].

Commentary

Cleanliness is very important during the prayer and outside prayer.
Therefore, there is an established habit of taking off shoes at Muslim
cultures in their homes and mosques in order to ensure cleanliness.
The above narration is an example how Rasulullah ﷺ was constantly
monitored by Allah سبحانه وتعالى in his life. The Divine instructions had
been revealing from Allah سبحانه وتعالى to establish the teachings of the
Quran in the practice and life of Rasulullah ﷺ. Immediately after the
demise of Rasulullah ﷺ, the theological schools[28] were structured by
the Muslim scholars. These schools systematized the teachings from
the Quran and from the life of Rasulullah ﷺ in order to increase the
accessibility of these guidelines for the following Muslim generations
at different times with different cultures. As the language of the Quran
and Hadith is originally in Arabic, these schools made these teachings
accessible especially among non-Arab Muslims. It is interesting to note
that only 10% (~200 million) of the Muslim population is native Arabs
and the rest are non-Arabs (~1.8 billion) [22].

---

28. mazhab

5. Abu Zarr asked to Rasulullah ﷺ: "Oh Prophet of Allah!, How about the person who loves a group of people but she or he cannot do what they do." The Prophet said: "Oh Abu Zarr! you will be with the people whom you love [1] [4].

Commentary

The above is a famous narration among Muslims. Abu Zarr is a person who is known to have an ascetic life. In practice, it is important to do good, ethical, and at the same time, believe and appreciate Allah سبحانه وتعالى sincerely and truly. Therefore, a person for whatever reason if they cannot do this, at least, having an affection and love for the people with these qualities can be the minimum requirement of being with this group of people in the afterlife. One of the ways to show this affinity and love is praying for these people. Another way is to talk good about these people.

6. One day Abu Haysam prepared a meal. Then, he invited Rasulullah ﷺ and the companions of Rasulullah ﷺ to enjoy the food. When they finished eating, Rasulullah ﷺ said: "Pay for the meal to your brother!" The companions said: "How do we pay him?" The Prophet replied: "When a person is invited to a house and enters into it, eats and drinks in that house, then this person prays for the house owner. This is the repayment of the house owner" [1].

Commentary

One of the etiquettes of thanking a person is praying for that person sincerely in Islam. There are a lot of encouragements in practice to pray for each other. When a person sincerely prays for the good of another person in this world and afterlife, then angels ask Allah سبحانه وتعالى to give the same type of good for the one who is praying. In other words, Allah سبحانه وتعالى gives good to both, the one who prays and the one who is prayed for.

7. What a loss is this person in! Then, what a loss is this person in! Then, unbelievably what a loss is this person in! Then, Rasulullah ﷺ was asked: "Who is this person oh Prophet of Allah?" The Prophet replied: "the person whose old parents either both of them or one of them were alive, but this person, the child, did not take care of them and did not enter Heaven by using this opportunity" [2] [2551].

Commentary

Allah سبحانه وتعالى gives in life different means for the person to enter Heaven. One of the easy ways of these means in Islam is to be nice to the parents and take care of them while they are alive. Parent's rights follow immediately after God's rights on the person in the clear teachings of the Quran and the Prophet Muhammad ﷺ. One of the easy ways to please God and enter to Heaven is to take care of the parents who are especially in need in their old age. The Prophet in the above narration alludes to this notion that a person is so unfortunate if he or she cannot use this means to be in Heaven by taking care of their old parents.

8. A man visited his brother in another town. Allah سبحانه وتعالى sent an angel in the form of a human to meet this man on his way. The angel said: "where are you going?" The man said: "I am going to visit my brother in this town." The angel said: "Are you going there to receive any type of benefit?" The man said: "No, I love him for the sake of Allah سبحانه وتعالى, the Glorified and the Majestic One." The angel said: "I am a messenger from Allah سبحانه وتعالى to tell you that Allah سبحانه وتعالى loves you as you love your brother for the sake of Allah" [2] (2567).

Commentary

In the testimony of Rasulullah ﷺ, the word is translated as brother. It can be a blood related brother or sister or it can be any friend that people can refer as brothers or sisters in human family. The above testimony shows the importance of loving each other for the sake of

Allah سبحانه وتعالى. A person may feel affinity with a person because the person may remind him or her about Allah سبحانه وتعالى and about the positive teachings of gratitude, appreciation, or virtue in one's relation with Allah سبحانه وتعالى and others . This type of engagement for some people can be a reason why a person can establish friendship, brother or sisterhood with another person. In this type of relation, God loves these worldly interest-free engagements. Therefore, Allah سبحانه وتعالى rewards the person in this life and in the afterlife with blessings and rewards.

---

9. The person who visits the sick is like the one who is in the fruit of garden of paradise until this person finishes the visit [2] (2568).

Commentary

When a person visits the sick and shows a kind sympathy for their suffering and pain, then Allah سبحانه وتعالى gives the reward and compensation to this person immediately with the through the feelings of satisfaction, peace and calmness in this world similar to pleasing feelings of being in paradise. Moreover, Allah سبحانه وتعالى gives immense rewards in the afterlife for this person. Therefore, there is a widespread practice of visiting the sick among Muslims.

---

10. The Prophet said: "Allah سبحانه وتعالى will say on the Day of Resurrection: "Oh child of Adam! I was sick but you did not visit Me." The person will reply: "Oh My Lord! How can I visit You? You are the Creator of all the worlds, galaxies and universes." Allah سبحانه وتعالى will say: "You knew a person who was sick but you did not visit and showed sympathy to this person. If you visited this person, you would then find Me there next to the sick." Allah سبحانه وتعالى will say: "Oh child of Adam! I asked food from you but you did not feed Me." The person will reply: "Oh My Lord! How can I feed You? You are the Creator of all the worlds, galaxies and universes." Allah سبحانه وتعالى will say: "You knew a person who was hungry but you did not feed this person. If you fed this person,

then you would find Me there next to the hungry and the one in need." Allah سبحانه وتعالى will say: "Oh child of Adam! I asked drink from you but you did not provide for Me." The person will reply: "Oh My Lord! How can I provide for You? You are the Creator of all the worlds, galaxies and universes." Allah سبحانه وتعالى will say: "You knew a person who was in need of drink and water but you did not provide for this person. If you quenched the thirst of this person and fulfilled this person's need, then you would find Me there next to the one in need" [2] (2569).

Commentary

One can see from the above testimony of Rasulullah ﷺ from Allah سبحانه وتعالى about humans' social, moral and fellowship responsibilities. The case of sickness shows the human responsibility of one to another in times of illness, tribulation and hardship. As human fellows, we cannot ignore the suffering of people around us. At least by visiting them and sharing with them with a few kind words, one can fulfil this basic responsibility according to the Islamic teachings. In the cases of scarcity of food and drink, one should share food, drink and water with the ones who are in need. In many sayings of Rasulullah ﷺ, there are a lot of narrations about altruism and not being selfish while others are suffering. In the above narration, one can see an example of a figurative language that is present in the scriptures.

11. Many with messy hair, covered with dust and not good looking people are turned away from doors and distanced from but if they were to adjure in the name of Allah ﷺ then, Allah ﷺ will certainly fulfil their wish [2] (2622).

Commentary

Above testimony of Rasulullah ﷺ underlines the importance of not judging people with their appearance, age, ethnicity, race or genders. In other words, our social norms can dictate who the good and beautiful people are but Rasulullah ﷺ instructs the real disposition of a person's heart and their relationship with Allah ﷻ adds value to the person's prominence but not their appearance. This is in such an extent that most of humans tend to judge with appearance and they make mistakes. If these discriminated people happened to pray Allah ﷻ and ask anything, then Allah ﷻ would for sure fulfill their wish. In another narration of Rasulullah ﷺ, Allah ﷻ is with the oppressed ones and fulfills the prayers of the oppressed [6]. In other words, when a person is discriminated, then this person is in reality oppressed. Therefore, Allah ﷻ immediately answers the prayers of this person due to oppression of discrimination.

---

12. The Arc Angel Gabriel insisted so much to me about the kind treatment of neighbors until I thought the neighbors would be included in one's will as one of the inheritors in the family [2] (2624).

Commentary

The above testimony of Rasulullah ﷺ shows the very kind treatment of neighbors as if they are one's family members. There are a lot of historical incidents in Islam due to the above statement of Rasulullah ﷺ that Muslims had been very careful, kind and gentle in their treatment of neighbors regardless of their faith.

---

13. Do not belittle anything from good, even if it can be a smiling and joyful countenance of your brother or sister [2] (2626).

Commentary

The above narration of Rasulullah ﷺ alludes to the importance of being always nice to others and making them comfortable in social encounters. One of the famous descriptions of Rasulullah ﷺ that he used to always have a smiling and pleasant face. He was always concerned about the genuine relationship of others.

14. The one who is not thankful to people will not be thankful to God
    (4811) [1]

Commentary

As one can see belief is an attitude of thankfulness according to the
above testimony of Rasulullah ﷺ. If a person does not show this attitude
towards people, he or she is less likely show it to the Creator. In another
perspective, if a person trains oneself with thankfulness to people there
is higher possibility that this person will be thankful to Allah ﷻ.

15. One day, a person was reprimanding his brother due to being
    modest and not sociable. The Prophet said: leave him alone,
    modesty is part of belief [1] (4795).

Commentary

Above testimony of Rasulullah ﷺ shows that sometimes society and
people expect us to behave in a certain way but if the person does not
follow these expectations then the person can be forced to follow these
norms. In this case of social life and modesty, a person can be shy from
people and may avoid social encounters. Then, this can be a positive
quality of a person when the person refrains due to possible harms
or embarrassments from people. Similarly, this can be a sign that this
person can have refraining qualities from the things that can displease
Allah ﷻ. This can be then a sign of one's belief in Allah ﷻ. The above
narration can be applied also in one's lifestyle. A person can be rich.
People can expect him or her to live a life with luxury according to this
person's wealth. T While others are living in lower living conditions, a
person in this case can have the qualities of modesty and shyness barring
him to live a wealthy life in order to emphatize with others.

16. Allah ﷻ certainly will help the person as long as this person is in the help of another human (believer) in a good cause and service [2] (2699).

Commentary

Above testimony of Rasulullah ﷺ is an encouragement for a person to do good for others. Today's grass root organizations about humanitarian aids, education, or medical care support are some of the examples that people engage themselves in order to receive the blessings from Allah ﷻ. In this sense, helping others becomes a religious act but not only ethical and moral disposition.

17. Ali reports that one day, Fatima, Ali's wife, who is also the daughter of Rasulullah ﷺ, was concerned for the soreness on her hand due to her regular usage of the hand mill. Then, she went to the house of Rasulullah ﷺ to seek if there was any maid to help her but she couldn't find Rasulullah ﷺ at his home so, she left. Then, she met Aisha, the wife of Rasulullah ﷺ and informed her about her need. After, Rasulullah ﷺ came, Aisha informed Rasulullah ﷺ about Fatima's visit. Then, Rasulullah ﷺ went to visit Fatima, his daughter, in her house. The Prophet found both Fatima and her husband Ali lying down in the bed. Ali continues and says: "To respect Rasulullah ﷺ's visit, we both tried to stand up from our bed but Rasulullah ﷺ said, "no need to get up, just stay how you are, be in your bed." Then, Rasulullah ﷺ sat down between us that I felt the coldness of his feet on my chest. Then, he said "Do you want me to inform you something better than what you asked? When you go to your bed, proclaim the greatness of Allah ﷻ 34 times (Allahuakbar), proclaim the glorification and perfectness of Allah ﷻ 33 times (SubhanAllah) and proclaim your gratitude and thanks to Allah ﷻ 33 times (Alhamdulillah'), then this better for you then a maid" [2] (2727).

Commentary

Above is the source of a widely practiced prayer before going to sleeping among Muslims. Before one sleeps, Rasulullah ﷺ advises to be in a state of connecting with Allah ﷻ with above chants and phrases of 34 times Allahuakbar, 33 times SubhanAllah, and 33 times Alhamdulillah. One should understand that Rasulullah ﷺ established a new community and society and he was the leader of them. People were coming with different needs and he was fulfilling their needs according to the available resources. In the above narration, if another person came to Rasulullah ﷺ other than his daughter, Fatima, perhaps Rasulullah ﷺ could have fulfilled their need immediately depending on the availability and their spiritual level. However, Rasulullah ﷺ himself practiced a level of piety with minimum attachment to the world, and desired the same disposition from his immediate family members as to be minimally involved with the worldly affairs of wealth, luxury, position and comfort. If Rasulullah ﷺ wanted, he could have lived in a luxurious living conditions. One day, one of the close friends of Rasulullah ﷺ, Omar came to visit him. He found Rasulullah ﷺ lying down and sleeping on the floor in a small room on a mat from bushes. When Omar saw this scene and saw the marks of bushes on his body, he started crying. Then, Rasulullah ﷺ woke up and asked him why he was crying. Omar said that all the kings in other countries were in their castles on comfortable beds and he was sleeping on a mat from bushes, although he had more power and access to the wealth and all the worldly means than them. The Prophet then said: "Oh Omar, let the world be theirs and afterlife will be ours [2]."

One can understand that Rasulullah ﷺ by choice avoided luxury and accumulating wealth. When there was wealth available, he immediately distributed among people. It is reported that most of the time Rasulullah ﷺ was hungry. On the other hand, Rasulullah ﷺ did not prohibit wealth and other means of world among his followers.

18. There is no person, a believer of Allah ﷻ, prays for his or her brother or sister in their absence and asks for their well-being from Allah ﷻ that angels say "Oh Allah! give and bless this person with the same well-being of their supplication, [2] (2732).

Commentary

When a person prays for others sincerely, Allah ☦ immediately rewards this person with the outcome of the same prayer. This is a divine teaching that even in one's prayers one should always think others. Humans' selfishness tendencies can also reveal themselves in their relationship with God. For example, one can always prefer to pray about him or herself to God about their needs. To prevent this intrinsic quality of a human being, the above testimony of Rasulullah ☦ encourages the person to also pray for the fulfillment of the needs of others as well as the for the needs of oneself. As a result, there is again a payback to the person in the form of angels praying for this person for the same good well-being.

19. Allah ☦ is pleased with the person when he or she eats food and thanks Allah ☦ for it and when he or she drinks beverage or water and thanks Allah ☦ for it [2] (2734).

Commentary

One of the practices that Muslims do is that before they start eating or drinking or before any good action they mention the name of Allah ☦ as bismillah. After they eat or drink, they thank Allah ☦ for it with the expression alhamdulillah. The essence of these expressions as explained in the Quran and by Rasulullah ☦ is that the person always should remember Allah ☦ in all parts of the daily discourses such as eating, going to bathroom, coming out of the bathroom, when being engaged in making decisions and other regular mundane activities. Then, after each engagement, thanking Allah ☦ for all the blessings is essential. In Islam, this is considered as one of the essences of the religious teachings in the form of daily prayers and rituals. In other words, the heart of five daily prayers is showing gratitude and thankfulness to Allah ☦ in different times of the day by verbal expressions of thankfulness, exaltation and perfection for Allah ☦ and by physical engagements of standing, bowing and prostration.

Art, Nature, Beauty, and Environment

Whoever is given flowers, should not reject them.
Certainly, flowers are easy to carry and pleasant in smell
[6].

1. Flowers

Whoever is given flowers, should not reject them. Certainly,
flowers are easy to carry and pleasant in smell [2].

Commentary

Although Rasulullah ﷺ lived a very simple life, he much valued good
smell, and scents. He did not eat himself the unpleasant odorful food
such as garlic or onion due to its smell although he allowed all the
followers, Muslims, to eat them [2]. There are various narrations about
a pleasant and nice smelling fragrant, musk, a type of pleasant smell
that spread from the clothes and body of Rasulullah ﷺ [2]. Therefore,
Muslims put on their bodies and clothes good smelling oils to emulate
Rasulullah ﷺ.

2. All the earth is a place of prayer except the graveyards, restrooms and bathrooms [1] (492) [4] (317).

Commentary

Two conditions for prayer are cleanliness of the body and the cleanliness of the place of worship. All the earth is clean. Therefore, entire earth is a place of worship and prayer for humans in Islam. It is more rewarding to go to a mosque to pray but it is not required. A person can pray in her or his home, office, school, car, garden, backyard, pavement, or at any place. The exception of graveyard is present due to the possible misunderstandings of people if they falsely establish the habit of worshiping the dead or deceased. The restroom exception is present due to the possible impurities and uncleanliness in restrooms and bathrooms.

3. I recognize the stone in Makkah. It used to greet me before I was sent as a messenger by Allah ﷻ. Now, I understand why it used to greet me [2] (2277).

Commentary

In Islam, everything recognizes and worships Allah سبحانه وتعالى except some of the humans and jinn. In the above narration, the stone had recognized Rasulullah ﷺ as the person of the chosen one who would be sent as a messenger of Allah سبحانه وتعالى. However, the Prophet Muhammad ﷺ was not a prophet at that time and he did not know all the details of the meanings and guidelines before the prophethood. As he was instructed with the divine guidelines and teachings, and received formal revelation from Allah سبحانه وتعالى through Arc Angel Gabriel, then the meanings of everything opened and revealed themselves in their full extent to Rasulullah ﷺ. One of the chapters of the Quran the chapter of dawn[29] mentions about this divine guidance of Rasulullah ﷺ by Allah سبحانه وتعالى.

---

29. Chapter number 93

4. Jabir bin Samura narrates that one day, I prayed the first noon prayer[30] with Rasulullah ﷺ. After, Rasulullah ﷺ left to see his family. I walked with him. The Prophet greeted the kids on the street one by one and patted their heads with a smile and Rasulullah ﷺ patted my head as well. I experienced a breeze of cool scent as if his hand was coming from a bottle of perfume [2] (2329).

Commentary

There are various narrations about the musk smell of Rasulullah ﷺ. The Prophet always encouraged applying scent and perfume to smell nice. Prayers, angelic beings, the creations of Allah سبحانه وتعالى all are nice and they are appealed and attracted to the clean and nice smelling people and environments. The Prophet himself often applied aromatic nice smelling oil on his body. Also, there are various narrations that Rasulullah ﷺ naturally smelt nice [2]. As a miracle from Allah سبحانه وتعالى, the sweat of Rasulullah ﷺ experienced by people that it was also smelling like nice perfume unlike other humans.

---

30. Zuhr

EPILOGUE

There are historical and biographical books about the life of the Prophet Muhammad ﷺ, Rasulullah ﷺ. As an alternative format, it is also important to learn the life of the Prophet Muhammad ﷺ through his statements, narration,s and sayings. Therefore, this book has some of the selected sayings and practices of the Prophet Muhammad ﷺ in a unique format especially including our present-day topics.

The goal of this book is to introduce Rasulullah ﷺ of Islam, the Prophet Muhammad ﷺ to all readers especially to the unfamiliar readers with the methodology of analyzing his statements, sayings, and practices. The statements, sayings, and practices of the Prophet Muhammad ﷺ are referred to as hadith as a technical term in Islam. So, hadith is different from the Quran. In Islamic theology, the Quran is the revelation of the book from Allah سبحانه وتعالى to the Prophet Muhammad ﷺ. Hadith is the sayings, statement,s and practices of the Prophet Muhammad ﷺ embodying the divine teachings. When one reviews both the Quran and the hadith, one can distinguish simply the different styles between the Quran and the sayings of Rasulullah ﷺ. The Quran gives main perspectives, then Rasulullah ﷺ explains the Quran in detail which is referred to as hadith. In the Western discourses, one can call the Quran as the main text and the hadith as the workbook of the belief and practice. As an example of this, one can find the longest chapter in this book on the subject of prayer that Rasulullah ﷺ explained how the prayer is expected to be embodied from the main teachings of the Quran.

One cannot understand the Quran correctly if there is no understanding and review of the hadith according to many scholars [23]. Therefore, Muslims have viewed both the Quran and the hadith at the same level of importance throughout the history of scholarship and practice [23].

In other words, both the Quran and the hadith are complementary to each other in Islam.

In this book, I have tried to use the six main book,s especially the ones accepted in the Muslim tradition for the sayings and practices of Rasulullah ﷺ. They are cited accordingly in the text. I used mainly the book of Sahih Muslim (referred to as As-Sahih Al-Muslim in Arabic). This book is especially suggested for academic studies because it presents different possibilities of the same hadith with a different chain of narrators with some similarities and differences. The hadith number is presented next to its citation with (round) parenthesis.

Yunus Kumek, PhD
Postdoctoral Fellow, Spring 2018
Harvard Divinity School

APPENDIX
Methodology of Studying the Hadith

Difference between the Quran and Hadith

It is important to differentiate the hadith from the Quran. Hadith are the sayings and practices of the Rasulullah 🕌, Prophet Muhammad 🕌. The Quran is the revelation, the book that was revealed to Rasulullah 🕌 in Islamic creed. In Islam, the Quran and the hadith have the highest power of the authentication of learning the religion for Muslims. Here are two examples among many from the Quran and the saying of Rasulullah 🕌 about Allah سبحانه وتعالى to allude to some of the textual and stylistic differences:

1. A Chapter of the Quran about Allah سبحانه وتعالى (Unity Chapter[31])

    In The Name of Allah, The Most Gracious, The Dispenser of Grace

    (1) **Say**: Allah is the One God:
    (2) Allah the Eternal, the Uncaused Cause of All Being.
    (3) Allah begets not, and neither is Allah begotten;
    (4) And there is nothing that could be compared with Allah [14]

---

31. Called chapter of unity or ikhlas in Arabic, 112th chapter.

2. Hadith about Allah سبحانه وتعالى

> Belief in Allah has more than 70 branches. The highest level as
> a sign of belief is accepting the statement that "there is no deity
> except only One God." The lowest sign of belief is to remove a
> harmful object on the road [5].

In the above circumstances, if one analyzes the reports about Allah
سبحانه وتعالى, the source reference of the first one is the Quran. The source
reference of the second one is the sayings of Rasulullah ﷺ referred as
hadith in its technical term. There is a clear textual and style distinction
between them. First, in the chapter of the Quran, there is the word "Say."
This word indicates that Allah سبحانه وتعالى tells the Prophet Muhammad
ﷺ as the messenger to deliver the message to people from Allah
سبحانه وتعالى. This word "Say" as an order comes immediately in the
beginning of this chapter. One can encounter this type of discourse
with the word "Say" in many places of the Quran addressing and
telling Rasulullah ﷺ to communicate the revealed message to the
people. Secondly, one can see very absolute and higher style of writing
as if giving a prescription similar to the commandments in biblical
traditions. In this case, God as the Transcendent Being communicates
with the creation through the scripture. On the other hand, one can see
a human's speech as a style and structure in the statement of Rasulullah
ﷺ as presented in the second case above.

Another difference is that the Quran was revealed from Allah
سبحانه وتعالى and has only one version as the Arabic revelation. The sayings
of Rasulullah ﷺ were recorded by early Muslims but have minor and
sometimes major variations in their recordings or chains. Therefore, the
hadith tradition, the science of authentication is developed. This science
studies and categorizes different types of narrations that can be more or
less authentic in its attribution to Rasulullah ﷺ. Whereas, the Quran
is one. There is no field of authentication for the Quran similar to the
sciences of hadith.

The sayings and practices of the Prophet Muhammad ﷺ are referred as
hadith. The hadith had been recorded both written and orally starting
immediately at the time of the Prophet Muhammad ﷺ [24]. Some of the

books have become famous in the compilations of the hadith traditions. Some of these books are As-Sahih Al-Bukhari, As-Sahih Al-Muslim, As-Sunan Al-Tirmidhi, As-Sunan Abu Dawud, As-Sunan Nasai, and As- Sunan Ibn Majah. Historically, the names of the books are referred to with the author's name respectively as Bukhari, Muslim, Tirmidhi, Abu Dawud, Nasai, or Ibn Dawud.

Methodology of Studying the Hadith

It is important to note that the sayings and practices of the Prophet Muhammad referred as hadith and sunnah, and are different from the Quran. If one analyzes the Quranic message and the hadith texts in their sentence structure, style, inclusivity or exclusivity, then one can realize the explicit and implicit differences between them. Even, this can be very apparent in their translated meanings. The Quran is in Arabic and there is only one version of the Quran.

However, the sayings of the Prophet Muhammad have many versions with different narrations by different people. Among these narrations, there is the classification of spectrum between the most authentic and the least authentic narrations.

Although one can see the multiplicity of versions or narrations, it is amazing to realize the meticulous methodology that was established immediately from the time of the Prophet Muhammad to classify the authentication levels of these narrations.

To give an example, if one takes one of the classical books of the narrations of the Prophet Muhammad , Sahih Muslim, then, one can find for the same a few line statements of Rasulullah that there can be up to ten, or more different narrations from different people recorded immediately after Rasulullah 's demise. For example, one can imagine hundreds of people sitting in the gathering of Prophet Muhammad , and some record with their recording tools and memorize them and some only memorize what they hear from the Rasulullah .

This knowledge is transmitted from the time of Rasulullah to our time very meticulously and carefully. In this transmission, both oral and written methodologies have beeb present to certify and authenticate the narrations from Rasulullah ﷺ. Therefore, studying the chain of the narrators and authentication procedures can be similar to gemology differentiating and leveling the validity. All these efforts have been established to ensure, and maintain the authenticity in Islamic knowledge.

Different people had recorded the statements of Rasulullah ﷺ the same way, or they recorded them with some differences. Each chain of narrations can signify different people who recorded a statement from Rasulullah ﷺ. Then, all these recordings are compiled as books starting immediately during the early generations of Islam [24].

For example, in the book of "Sahih Muslim", the name of the author of the book is given as the book title. The collector's name is Muslim. Sahih Muslim can translate as "the authentic compilations of Muslim." He complied and wrote this book by including different narrations with different chains.

To allude to this process of narrations in the science of hadith, below is an example of narrations for the same saying of Rasulullah ﷺ:

Hadith A: "Certainly, all the deeds are rewarded according to their intentions."

Let's call this saying of Rasulullah ﷺ as the version A which is the most narrated and the most authentic saying of Rasulullah ﷺ on this particular narration.

Hadith A': "All the deeds are rewarded according to their intentions."

In this version, the word "certainly" is missing compared to the version A.

Hadith A": "All the deeds and actions are rewarded according to their intentions."

The word "actions" is extra compared to the version A.

Now, let's look at different people with different chain of narrators narrating the versions A, A' or A" narrations. These chains of narrators are below:

A → Chain 1: Prophet Muhammad → Fatima → Abraham → John → Muslim (the compiler)

A → Chain 2: Prophet Muhammad → Fatima → Moses → Mark → Muslim (the compiler)

A' → Chain 3: Prophet Muhammad → Isaac → Jennifer → Mark → Muslim (the compiler)

A" → Chain 4: Prophet Muhammad → Abu Hurayra → Jonah → John → Muslim (the compiler)

Statement A is narrated through chain 1 and chain 2. It is the same statement of Rasulullah 🌸 but different chain of narrations. Also, with a slight change in the saying of Rasulullah 🌸, there are two different versions A' and A" with chains 3 and 4.

This is summarized in the diagram below:

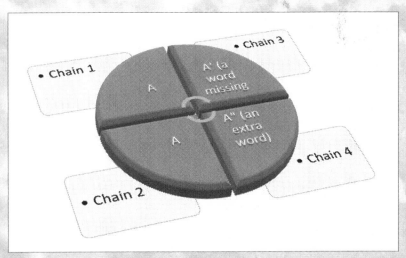

FIGURE 1

Example for the science of narrations in the discipline of hadith.

BIBLIOGRAPHY

[1] S. b. Ash'ath, Sunan Abu Dawud, riyadh: Darussalam, 2008.

[2] A. Muslim, Sahih Muslim (translated by Siddiqui, A.), Peace Vision, 1972.

[3] A. Tabarani, Kitab Ad-Du'a, Darul Hadis, 2014.

[4] M. Tirmizi, Jami At-Tirmizi, Dar-us-Salam, 2007.

[5] I. Majah, Sunan Ibn Majah.

[6] M. Al-Bukhari, The translation of the meanings of Sahih Al-Bukhari, Kazi Publications, 1986.

[7] S. Vahide, The Collection of Light, ihlas nur publication, 2001.

[8] Y. J. Kumek, Practical Mysticism: Sufi Journeys of Heart and Mind, Dubuque: Kendall Hunt, 2018.

[9] A. An-Nasa'i, Sunan An-Nasai, Riyadh: Daraussalalm, 2007.

[10] A. B. Hanbal, Musnad Imam Ahmad Ibn Hanbal, Dar-Us-Salam Publications, 2012.

[11] J. B., Interviewee, *Anthropologial Field Notes with New Comers.* [Interview]. 11 June 2007.

[12] M. Tirmizi, Jami At-Tirmizi, Salat 13 (171).

[13] Y. Kumek, Selected Passages from the Quran, Dubuque, Iowa: KendalHunt, 2018, p. 67.

[14 M. Asad, The message of the Quran: Translated and explained., Al-Andalus Gibraltar, 1980.

[15] W. Musaad, Interviewee, *Rihla 2018.* [Interview]. 3 July 2018.

[16] C. Melchert, "God Created Adam in His Image," *Journal of Qur'anic Studies,* vol. 13, no. 1, pp. 113–124, 2011.

[17] T. Ramadan, In the Footsteps of the Prophet: Lessons from the Life of Muhammad, Oxford University Press, 2009.

[18] J. A. Brown, Slavery & Islam, Oneworld Publications, 2019.

[19] M. i. I. Bukhārī, UK Islamic Academy, 2005.

[20] H. Khattab, Bent Rib: A Journey Through Women's Issues in Islam, International Islamic Publishing House, 2007.

[21] O. Pamuk, Istanbul: Memories and the City, Alfred A. Knopf, 2017.

[22] J. L. Esposito, What Everyone Needs to Know about Islam, Oxford University Press, 2011.

[23] J. A. C. Brown, Hadith: Muhammad's Legacy in the Medieval and Modern World, Oneworld Publications, 2009.

[24] I. Memon, The Preservation of Hadith, NY: Madania Publications, 2010.

[25] U. P. Oxford, "Oxford Dictionaries," 2016. [Online]. Available: http://www.oxforddictionaries.com/us/definition/american_ english/. [Accessed 2016].

GLOSSARY

Allah: The Proper Name of Creator in Islam, translated as God in English

Allah سبحانه وتعالى: The Proper Name of Creator in Islam, translated as God in English. The addition Arabic phrase سبحانه وتعالى reads as Subhanahu Wa Ta'ala and abbreviated as (SWT). A phrase of respect for the glory and perfection of God when the name of God as Allah is mentioned or stated.

A'bd: worshipper, servant, or slave

Accountability: liability, especially in Sufism and in Abrahamic traditions, everyone has a free will or agency in this world but accountability for their actions in the afterlife in front of God

Adab: good manners, esp. in the relationship with God in Sufism

Adjective: attribute, a phrase describing a noun

Adonai: name of God in Judaism

Agency: acting as an agent or a carrier with free will

Alhamdulillah: a chanted divine phrase of appreciation of God or Allah

Alienating: isolating, separating, disconnecting

Alienating Images of God: Understandings about God that disconnects person to establish a regular relationship with the Divine or to follow a religion

Allah: proper name of God in Islam

Allude: explain, refer

Anger: uncontrolled and chaotic human spiritual state

Aphorism: sayings, proverbs in a culture,ociet,y or belief

Appreciate: thank

Appreciative: with capital A, God

Arabic: language, especially the language of revelation of the Quran

Arrogance: feelings and actions of superiority

Assert: claim

Astagfirullah: a divine phrase of asking forgiveness from God and cleaning the heart

Attribute: adjective, a phrase describing a noun, especially in Sufism, attributes of God: divine phrases describing God

Authentic: original, genuine, true

Balance: modesty, especially in Sufism, following the middle way

Behavior: temporary nature of a person

Bismillah: a divine phrase of starting something with the blessing of God

Boost: increase

Bowing down: bending one's body, especially the act of respect by bending one's body, for God

Certainty: knowing without doubt, especially in Sufism, knowing and experiencing without doubt

Chanting: repeating, especially in Sufism, repeating the phrases with focus and experience

Chaos: disorder and confusion, especially in Sufism (spiritual) chaos being in negative states of anxiety, stress, and purposelessness

Compassion: loving and caring

Conscience: internal instinct of distinguishing right or wrong

Consciousness: awareness

Constant: not changing, permanent, especially in practice, known as Reflective Attributes of God, where humans have an image but God has its source

Construction: formation of an abstract entity

Contract: squeeze

Convergence: similarity

Cosmology: knowledge about the origin and development of the universe

Covenant: agreement

Death: end of physical faculties of a person, especially physical versus spiritual death; the soul does not die but the body dies in understanding of physical death in Islam

Dedication: sincere constant effort

Deity: representation of the transcendent

Detox: discharge

Devout: pious, practicing

Dhikr: as one of the names of the Quran, or any type of chant to remember God

Discharge: negative states of spirituality that makes the person sad, stressed, and anxious, especially in Sufism, emptying oneself from all the temporal and worldly positive and negative attachments

Divine: transcendent

Doctrine: teaching

Dominance: control

Dream: visions when one is sleeping or awake

Ego: self, identifier of a person, especially in Sufism, raw and uneducated identifier and controller of a person

Elohim: name of God in Judaism

Embodiment, versus embody: making it part of one's character

Endeavor: engagement, activities

Epistemology: theory of knowledge

Ethical: moral

Ethnographic: based on observation

Etiquette: good manners and respect, especially in Sufism, respect in the relationship with God

Evil: anything that causes stress, sadness, or anxiety

Evil eye: the belief of unknown effects of the human eye across different cultures, tradition,s and religions, especially in Sufism the evil eye effects due to extreme hatred, jealousy, or, oppositely, evil eye effects due to extreme veneration and love of someone

Expand: enlarge

Experience: internalization of knowledge

Experience or experiential knowledge: all types of learning except from a book or a teacher, internalizing and personalizing the formal learning

Figurative: unclear, secondary, and metaphorical

Free Will: free choice of a person in decision-making

Generous: with capital G, God

Genre: type

Genuine: sincere, original, authentic

Ghazali: philosopher, theologician, Sufi mystic, lived in 12th century

Glorification: the mental, spiritual, and maybe verbal act of describing God in an admirable way

Groundless: fake

Habitual: habit of doing something constantly

HasbiyaAllah: a chant with a meaning of "God is sufficient for me"

Healthy Cookies: beneficial extraordinary incidents, such as miracles in Sufism

Heaven: a place of all maximized pleasures of bodily and spiritual engagements while being with God

Hell: a place of punishment

Heretic: abnormal person, especially in Sufism, a desired state of being to experience and know the Divine

Humbleness: behavior of modesty in viewing oneself, especially in Sufism, accepting the weakness in one's relationship with God and not being disrespectful and arrogant to God

Humility: character or trait of humbleness

Illa Allah: "except Allah" or "except God"

Images of God: understandings and experiences about God

Imitation: trying without real understanding

Infinite: God, the Unlimited

Informant: a person who participates in anthropological research

InshAllah: God willing, hopefully

Intention: planning ideas before the action

Internalize: making it part of one's character, trait or nature in Sufism

Intrinsic: internal

Isa: Jesus in Arabic as mentioned in the Quran. The Arabic phrase عليه السلام is a phrase of respect that Muslims say when the name of Jesus (Isa) is mentioned or stated.

Islam: name of a religion that emphasizes believing in one God and Jesus, Moses, and Muhammad to be the human prophets of the Creator

Jihad: struggle, esp. spiritual struggle within oneself

Joseph: Prophet of God in Islam, Christianity, and Judaism

Khidr: mystical being who is sent by God at any time to help people in their problems; also believed to be the teacher of Moses in a mystical journey as mentioned in the Quran

Kitab: the Quran

Knowledge: theoretical understanding of something through education

La ilaha illa Allah: there is no God except Allah, a critical Divine phrase of chanting in Sufism implying a spiritual charge and discharge

Literal: clear and primary

Lord: God

Lucifer: Satan, mentioned in divine scriptures such as the Bible and the Quran

Meditation: deep focus especially with reflection

Memorization: learning by heart

Mercy: compassion and forgiveness

Middle way: living a balanced life in spiritual and worldly engagements

Mimic: imitate

Mind: logic, reason, and rationality

Miracle: incidents against the law of physics and against all natural sciences

Muhammad: the Prophet of Islam, referred as "Rasulullah ﷺ" or the Prophet" in the text

Musa: The name of Moses in Arabic as mentioned in the Quran. The Arabic phrase عليه السلام is a phrase of respect that Muslims say when the name of Moses (Musa) is mentioned or stated.

Musaddiq: the Quran

Nafs: self in its raw form

Neat: tidy and in order

Negation: denial, esp. in Sufism, emptying from the mind and heart the imperfect ideas and feelings about God

Neglectful: not giving the proper attention that is due

Notion: concept, idea

Odd: not even, unique, no equivalence

One: with capital denoting the one and only Creator

Oppression: unjust action of the strong over the weak

Permanent: constant, not changing, not ending

Phenomenon: occurrence

Pious: devout, practicing

Popular culture: the ethnographic data gathered over the period of years among different Sufi communities

Pronunciation: correct sounds of letters in a language

Prophet: Muhammad, the Prophet of Islam, referred as "the Prophet" or "Rasulullah ﷺ" in the text

Prostration, versus to prostrate: the act of respect by putting one's face on the ground, especially in Sufism, humbling oneself for God by putting the face, the noble part of the body, on the ground

Qibla: the direction where Muslims and Sufis turn when they pray

Quran: sacred text of Muslims

Rasulullah: the Prophet Muhammad. This phrase translates as the messenger of God.

Rasulullah ﷺ: the Prophet Muhammad. This phrase translates as the messenger of God. The additional phrase of respect in Arabic ﷺ transliterates as "Sallalahu Alayhi Wa Sallam" abbreviated as (SAWS). This is to be said when the name of the Prophet is stated or mentioned.

Recitation, versus to recite: reading, versus to read

Reliance: dependence

Repetition: repeating

Reverence: respect

Reward: prize, payment, especially in worldly and afterlife rewards in Islam

Ritual: practices in a religion or mysticism that have spiritual and divine value for a person

Ruku: bowing down

Rumi: great Sufi mystic

Saint: the person believed to be close to God

Sakina: peaceful and calm feelings

Salawat: names of the chants to remember teachers and their covenants with their students, especially the main teacher, the Prophet Muhammad ﷺ and others, such as Abraham, Moses, and Jesus

Samad: the One who does not need anything, but everyone and everything needs God

Satan: the Devil, Lucifer, mentioned in divine scriptures such as in the Bible and the Quran

Scent: perfume, nice smell

Scholar: expert, especially in Sufism, the experts who practice what they teach (alim)

Scripture: sacred book or sacred text

Self: ego, identifier of a person, especially in Sufism, raw and uneducated identifier and controller of a person

Service: ethical action of doing good for others and society

Spiritual Journey: struggles of following guidelines of a mystical school

State: level, especially in Sufism, spiritual level

Struggle: efforts to achieve a goal

SubhanAllah: glorification of God, a divine phrase of chanting of spirituality implying a spiritual charge and discharge

SubhanAllahu wa bihamdihi: a divine phrase of glorification of God

SubhanAllahul Azeem: a divine phrase of glorification of God in the prostration posture

SubhanRabbiyalAzim: phrase of glorification for God in the bowing posture

Submission: natural acceptance of the uncontrolled and unseen

Sufi: follower of Sufism

Sufism: mystical path of Islam

Superstitious: fake

Surrender: involuntary state of acceptance of the uncontrolled and the unseen

Tahajjud: night prayer

Talismanic: unknown and indescribable effects of divine words and sounds

Taqwa: respect of God

Taste: pleasure, especially spiritual pleasure such as peace, calmness, joy, and happiness in Sufism

Temple: worship place

Temporal: ending

Temporary: transitory

Temptation: false ideas

The Curer: God

The Divine: God

The Forgiver: a name of God in Sufism

The Friend: a name of God in Sufism

The Helper: a name of God in Sufism

The Lover: a name of God in Sufism

The Peace Giver: God

The Prophet: Muhammad, the Prophet of Islam, referred as "the Prophet" or "Rasulullah ﷺ"

The Real: God

The Real Maker: God

The Source: God

The Sustainer: a name of God in Sufism

The Reminder: the Quran

The Wise: with capital W, God

Throne: a figurative or metaphorical representation of dominion of God

Trait: permanent character or nature

Tranquility: peace and calmness

Transcendent: beyond human limits

Transitory: temporal

Transliteration: writing the sounds of words or phrases in one language with an alphabet of another language

Union: being together, especially in this book, goal and joy of being always in the presence of God

Unseen: anything five senses cannot testify in scientific methods

Weak: not having a physical strength to perform an action, especially in Sufism, not having spiritual strength to perform any action

Worshipper: a person who regularly follows and practices rituals, acts of prayers

ACKNOWLEDGMENTS

I would like to thank all my unnamed teachers, friends, and students for their input, ideas, suggestions, help, and support during and before the preparation of this book.

I would like to thank Dr. David Banks, faculty of the Department of Anthropology, State University of New York (SUNY) at Bufalo, for meeting with me daily to go over the manuscript. I would like to also thank Sister Erica for all her editing and suggestions and comments. Lastly, I would like to thank all of my family members for their patience with me during the preparation of this book.

AUTHOR BIO

Dr. M. Yunus Kumek is currently teaching at Harvard Divinity School on Islam. He has been religious studies coordinator at State University of New York (SUNY) Buffalo State and teaching undergraduate and graduate courses in religious studies at SUNY at Buffalo State, Niagara University and Daemen College. Before becoming interested in religious studies, Dr. Kumek was doing his doctorate degree in physics at SUNY at Buffalo published academic papers in the areas of quantum physics and medical physics. Then, he decided to engage with the world of social sciences through social anthropology, education, and cultural anthropology in his doctorate studies and subsequently, spent a few years as a research associate in the anthropology department of the same university. Recently, he completed a postdoctoral fellowship at Harvard Divinity school and published books on religious literacy through ethnography and selected passages from the Quran with interpreted contextual meanings. Dr. Kumek had classical training in Islamic sciences from the teachers of Egypt, India, Turkey, Yemen, Somalia, Morocco, and the United States. He stayed and studied in Egypt and Turkey. Dr. Kumek, who remains interested in physics—solves physics problems to relax—enjoys different languages: German, Spanish, Arabic, Urdu, and Turkish, especially in his research of scriptural analysis. Dr. Kumek takes great pleasure in classical poetry as well.

INDEX

65940983R00109

Made in the USA
Middletown, DE
04 September 2019